HOMEWORK
WITHOUT TEARS

HOMEWORK WITHOUT TEARS

Lee Canter and Lee Hausner, Ph.D.

HarperPerennial
A Division of HarperCollins*Publishers*

This book was originally published by Canter & Associates, Inc., in 1987.

Designer: Tom Winberry
Illustrator: Bob McMahon
Photographer: Cliff Kramer

Library of Congress Catalog Card Number 88-45109
ISBN 0-06-273132-7 (pbk.)

97 98 99   RRD   20 19 18 17 16 15 14 13 12 11

ACKNOWLEDGMENTS

The skills and ideas of many people have been invaluable in the development of this book. We would like to thank the following educators, parents and Canter and Associates, Inc., staff for their contributions and support.

Dr. Elden Barrett
Linda and Leonard Cohen
Dr. Judy Cooper
Diana Geddes-Day
Terry Garnholz
Mark Falstein
Fred Lilly
Margaret MacKinnon
Joan McClintic
Ron Pearson
Dale Petrulis
Joe Presutto
Carol Provisor
Simone Reiswig
Martha Richey
Helene Robbins
Janet Robinson
Sandi Searls
Barbara Schadlow
Marcia Shank
Bert Simmons
Mary Jo Swartley
Jim Thompson
Kathy Winberry

CONTENTS

INTRODUCTION

Our son Josh came to us one evening with a series of questions he was supposed to answer for homework. When neither of us could help with the answers, we asked to see his textbook. Sure enough, the answers to all of the questions could be found in the appropriate chapter.

When we asked our son about this, he shrugged, "The teacher said to answer the questions. She didn't say we had to read the chapter, too."

Both our son and daughter are very good students, but they are also very normal children. And if there is anything that all children love to avoid doing, it is homework.

Over the past years, we have written several books about behavior management for both parents and teachers. Recently, someone asked what the subject of our next book was going to be. When we said homework, the remark was, "Homework? Homework is important and kids should do it."

Yes, it is important that your children do their homework. The question is how to accomplish this without tears—yours or your children's.

As our children progressed through school, we began looking at how we as parents might be able to help our children succeed in school. It didn't take us long to realize that the one area where we could have a direct and significant impact was homework.

Unfortunately, homework is usually looked at as something teachers give, children do and parents endure. At best, homework is usually something we parents take for granted. At worst, it is the subject of nightly confrontations with tearful resolutions.

Why is homework such a problem for parents and children? The problem is that parents know the importance of homework, but they don't know how to deal with their children when doing homework becomes a problem.

What do you do now when you hear:

> "I'll do my homework after I go out and play for just a little while."

> "My report's due tomorrow and you've just got to help me."

> "It's too quiet to work with the TV off."

If those types of comments are all too familiar, this book can be of help to you.

For years, we have been helping teachers help children to become more responsible classroom learners. We have developed a program used by over one-half million teachers to help students make good choices about how they behave in the classroom.

In this book, we have taken that same program and applied it to homework. In addition, we have included the results of research about study skills that parents can teach children to help them succeed.

If you are thinking that this is going to take some effort on your part, you are right. But homework is going to take your time and effort one way or another. And if it is going to take that time, wouldn't it be better if it was a positive experience for both you and your children?

The objective of this book is to make the time spent with children about homework positive and rewarding for both of you. For parents, homework is an opportunity to help your children succeed in school. For children, it is an opportunity, perhaps for the first time, to take some responsibility for their own lives and feel good about succeeding at something important.

As parents, we all want to help our children to do well in school, develop a good self image and gain the confidence they need to become responsible, productive adults. Our hope is that this book will help you help your children to do just that.

P.S. Josh, by the way, hasn't missed reading a chapter since we zeroed in on the problem. He's an excellent student and is serving as a great role model for his younger sister Nicole. We're very proud of both of them.

Lee and Marlene Canter

HOMEWORK
WITHOUT TEARS

WHAT IS HOMEWORK WITHOUT TEARS?

What Is Homework Without Tears?

Do any of these situations occur in your home?

☐ You and your children engage in nightly battles over when homework will be done.

☐ Your children rush through homework assignments, with sloppy, incomplete results.

☐ Your children "forget" to bring their homework assignments home.

☐ You do more of the homework than your children do.

☐ Your children take forever to finish their homework assignments.

☐ Your children insist that they are able to do homework while watching TV, talking on the phone, and listening to the stereo.

☐ The first time you hear about a major project is the night before it's due . . .and it isn't finished.

If you answered "yes" to any of the above, then you have felt the frustration many parents feel when dealing with homework. *Homework Without Tears* was written for you.

How many times have you wished that there was something you could do to help your children deal more successfully with homework? How often have you searched for just the right words or just the right actions to end your family's nightly homework battles forever? If you're like most parents, you've tried a lot of different strategies—off and on— only to find you and your children falling back into the same ineffective routines. You know that your children need to do their homework, and you want to help, but you just aren't sure how to go about it.

Relax. You can do it. You have the power to turn around the homework situation in your home and motivate your children to succeed academically.

Your children, of course, are the ones who must do the work—and do it appropriately. But you are the one who can help make it all possible. The *Homework Without Tears* program is based on the research-supported fact that your interest and involvement are the keys to your children's success in school—and that one of the most effective ways you can be involved in their education is through homework. The steps you must take to create an environment conducive to doing homework are outlined in this book. The effectiveness of these steps, and of the *Homework Without Tears* program, depends upon the attitude you consistently project about homework.

You've already demonstrated your interest by beginning to read this book. The next step is to turn this interest into result-getting action by letting your children know exactly where you stand on the issue of education—and homework.

As you read this chapter, you will see that homework has been proven to be a powerful tool for ensuring your children's success in school. Research supports that fact. Your goal then, must be to use this tool to its best advantage. You have to begin looking at homework as **a daily opportunity to have a positive impact on your children's education and future.** You must convey to your children the message that you believe in them—that you are committed to their success and that homework is an important part of that commitment.

Because we believe that your commitment and enthusiasm are vital to your children's success in school, we begin the *Homework Without Tears* program by taking a closer look at why homework is so important—and why your involvement is so necessary.

Homework affects achievement in school.

As a parent, it's important for you to know that homework really does make a difference in your children's performance at school. Research tells us that the time spent doing homework *directly affects* a child's achievement. This is important information. It tells us that by doing assigned homework, children will increase skills and do better in school. Some recent findings:

Students who consistently do homework perform better academically than those who do not do homework.

By doing homework, students can improve academic achievement in all subjects.

Homework improves academic achievement at all grade levels, both elementary and secondary.

Doing homework improves academic achievement of both high and low achievers.

When you help your children do their homework appropriately, you are helping them improve academically. Through homework, you have the daily opportunity to make your children more successful.

Homework teaches your children responsibility.

When your children were very young, you made most of their decisions for them. You structured their activities, planned their meals, and made sure they got to bed on time. Even when you began to guide them into making choices of their own, you still probably kept very close tabs on what those choices were. When your children first began school, their teacher offered much of the same guidance.

Until homework. For many children, homework is the first time they have a responsibility all their own. It's up to them to bring it home. It's up to them to do the work. And it's up to them to see that the work gets back to school. From the moment the teacher gives the assignment to the moment it is turned in again, the responsibility rests on your children's shoulders. It is important for you to realize that this is a responsibility that has a tremendous impact on your children's lives. Why such an impact?

Through homework, children learn skills that they must develop if they are to grow to be independent, motivated and successful adults. They learn to follow directions, work on their own, begin and complete a task, manage their time, and work to their full potential.

They learn that it's up to them—that they are accountable for their own actions. If you as a parent fail to reinforce the importance of homework, then you are denying them the chance to fully develop this sense of responsibility.

Keep these benefits in mind, especially when your children are given homework assignments which to you (and them) seem to be meaningless busywork. Don't dismiss this homework as unimportant. It's teaching your children something valuable! Life, after all, is filled with sometimes tiresome details that must be dealt with appropriately. Keep in mind that you and your children are laying a foundation that they will build upon for years to come.

Homework is the key link between home and school.

Homework is the best means you have of maintaining a day-to-day connection with your child's education. Since homework is assigned on a regular basis, it can provide almost continuous contact between you, your child, and your child's teacher.

Why is this contact so important? Read on . . .

Which of the following do you think is the most crucial element in determining a child's success in school?

    a. teacher competence and guidance
    b. the amount of money the government spends on
       education
    c. parents' motivation and support

The answer to the question is "c." Parents' motivation and support are the most important factors in determining whether a child will do well in school. Virtually every report on education issued over the last twenty years has come to the same conclusion. Children can suffer incompetent teachers without losing their eagerness for learning. They can survive rock-bottom school budgets, inadequate textbooks and antiquated facilities without giving up on education altogether. But without parental support, without encouragement, motivation, and discipline on the home front, children are almost certain to develop a negative attitude toward learning and school. The successful students all seem to have parents whose attitudes show they care about their children's schoolwork. You can demonstrate how you feel about education by taking a stand. You can let your children know that their education is a priority in your family. And homework is a part of that priority.

Nearly every day, most students are assigned some form of schoolwork to be done at home. Thus, on a daily basis, through the importance you place on homework, you can show your children your commitment to their success in school. *Homework Without Tears* will show you how to make that commitment.

Your children's success is in your hands.

We know that it's tough for parents to hear about the problems facing schools today. The news is filled with stories of overcrowded campuses, controversy over curriculum, insufficient budgets, and poor test scores—all of which may make parents wonder where their children's education is headed. It's easy to feel frustrated—but you must never feel powerless. You can't change the schools overnight, but through your involvement you can change the direction of your children's education. Remember, the best schools are ones that have the support of the families they serve. When you support homework, you strengthen the school's programs and their effectiveness. Everybody benefits—parents, teachers, and especially the students.

Your children's age and current success in school will dictate the level of your involvement. With younger children you must be prepared to be Involved on a dally basls. Working Independently Is a learned— and practiced—skill. It takes some time and patience. But if you build a solid foundation of good study habits when your children are young, you will find that your children will be able to work independently when they are older.

Likewise, if your children are older, but have not developed appropriate study habits, you are going to have to back up a bit and help them learn what it means to work responsibly. *Homework Without Tears* gives you guidelines throughout the program that will help you determine the level of your involvement at each step along the way.

Don't worry –you're *not* the teacher.

The *Homework Without Tears* program does not require you to take on the role of teacher. It is not your responsibility to teach your children concepts or to correct their work. It's not your job. Besides, it's counterproductive. It causes conflicts instead of resolving them. The idea is to make things easier for you and your child, not harder.

Homework Without Tears does guide you in establishing a disciplined, supportive learning environment in your home. You don't need a teaching credential or a degree in psychology. All you have to do is put the program into action!

WHAT HOMEWORK WITHOUT TEARS WILL DO FOR YOU

Through *Homework Without Tears* you will learn:

How to set up a proper study area.

Your children cannot do their homework in a distracting environment. The first step you must take in helping your children do their homework successfully is to see that they have a proper study area in which to work. *Homework Without Tears* will teach you how to set up a proper study area in your home.

How to get homework finished on time.

Getting homework finished on time is a big problem in many families. That's because all too often homework is the last thing scheduled into a child's life. Soccer, dance lessons, Little League and Scouts are attended faithfully . . . and punctually. Homework is often just "squeezed in." This kind of "system" doesn't work. The homework gets attended to at the last minute, and your child gets the message that other activities are more important. *Homework Without Tears* will show you how to turn this situation around. You will learn how to schedule homework time and how to give your children the clear message that in your home, homework is their number-one priority.

How to get your children to do homework on their own.

Homework teaches children responsibility. But this responsibility cannot be learned if your children never really work on their own. Through *Homework Without Tears* you will learn techniques and tips to encourage your children to work independently.

How to motivate your children with praise.

When children feel good about themselves, they feel more motivated to do well in school. When you praise your children's efforts, you are saying to them, "We believe in you, and in your ability." This has a tremendous impact on children. *Homework Without Tears* will teach you how to effectively motivate your children with praise.

How to motivate your children to do their best work.

For some children, even words of praise just aren't enough. These children need a little extra incentive to initiate their enthusiasm about doing homework. *Homework Without Tears* offers a variety of motivating ideas for all ages.

How to communicate assertively with your children.

Your children must understand that you are serious about homework being completed appropriately. But if you beg, speak angrily to, or argue with your kids, they'll just turn off. You must learn to *communi-*

cate assertively—to say what you mean, and mean what you say. It will make the difference between children who listen, and children who don't. *Homework Without Tears* will give you the techniques you need to become an assertive parent!

How to back up your words with action.

When your children consistently refuse to do their homework, it's time to take action. But this doesn't mean screaming, yelling, or threatening your children with punishment. It simply means that you are going to give your children a choice. They can choose to do homework appropriately, or they can choose to lose privileges. It's as simple as that. *Homework Without Tears* will teach you skills you need to maintain this position of strength and resolve. You can do it! Remember, in your home, homework is a number-one priority. Your children *will* do their homework!

How to work with your children's teacher.

You and your children's teacher must work together as a team—a team that is committed to your children's progress. The secret to building and maintaining that relationship is through communication. *Homework Without Tears* will give you guidelines about when and how to contact your children's teacher.

How to provide study skills that will improve your children's performance at school.

Very often the difference between successful students and unsuccessful ones is that successful students know how to study. They know how to organize their time, how to study for tests, how to get the most from what they read, and how to write papers. These students have developed skills that enable them to use their study time to their best advantage. As a result, they do better in school. We call these skills *study skills*. Study skills are techniques that enable students to learn more effectively. *Homework Without Tears* provides a set of study skills that will help your children do their homework — and assignments in class — more effectively. *Homework Without Tears* will show you:

How to help your children improve reading skills.

How to help your children become better spellers.

How to help your children plan long-range projects.

How to help your children write a term report.

How to help your children study information in
a textbook.

How to help your children proofread their work.

The *Homework Without Tears* program will work for you. It's simply a matter of attitude, action, and support. As you read this book and start to put the program into action, you'll recognize that getting your children to do homework does not have to threaten the peace of your family.

There is something you can do. With *Homework Without Tears*, your children can soon be on their way to success, and the family can get on to a more peaceful coexistence. There's nothing to it but to do it.

HOMEWORK MUST BE DONE IN A PROPER STUDY AREA

Homework Must Be Done in a Proper Study Area

To do homework successfully, your children must have a quiet place in which to work. They simply cannot do their homework effectively in a distracting environment. They cannot do it in front of a TV set. They cannot do it while talking on the telephone. They cannot do it if they are constantly being bothered by brothers and sisters. Homework must be done in a quiet place. It is your responsibility to help your children find an appropriate place in which to do homework.

It's not difficult to set up a proper study area. Your children do not need a lot of space to do homework. What they do need is a well-lit, comfortable, quiet location with all necessary supplies at hand. Once they get into the habit of working in an appropriate area, their attitude toward homework will change. They may not notice it at first, but their efficiency and attention span will increase almost at once. Homework will seem easier for them. And it will certainly seem easier for you.

HOW TO SET UP A PROPER STUDY AREA

Tell your children that they must have a special place where they will do homework.

"We want you to do your homework in a quiet place where you'll be able to concentrate. To help make sure you'll have the quiet you need, we'll work with you to decide on a good spot for your homework area. Maybe it will be in your room, maybe the kitchen table. But wherever we decide, it will be your homework space during the time you're doing your homework. No one will be allowed to disturb you or to interfere. TV, radio, and stereo will be kept off in your homework area because they interfere, too."

Choose a location where your child will do homework.

It doesn't matter where your child does homework, as long as the location is free from distraction.

Follow these guidelines for choosing a proper study area:	
Grades K-3	You and your child should choose the location together. Make sure it is some place close where you can be available for help.
Grades 4-6	Guide your child in choosing a good location. Talk together about which places in your home might be better than others for doing homework.
Grades 7-12	Your child can choose his* own work space. But make sure it meets the distraction-free criteria.

Make sure that the space is well lit.

Research indicates that poor lighting increases eye fatigue by fifty percent.

Post a "DO NOT DISTURB" sign during homework time.

Experience teaches us that every time your children are interrupted, it takes them two to three minutes to regain their concentration. A "Do Not Disturb" sign (page 141 of the Appendix) lets everyone in the family know that interruptions are not allowed!

Equip your child's work space with a Homework Survival Kit.

A Homework Survival Kit should contain all the materials children need to do their homework. It prevents your children from being continually distracted by the need to go searching for supplies.

---

* Because the English language does not have a pronoun that applies to both sexes, we have alternated the use of masculine and feminine pronouns in the different chapters of *Homework Without Tears*.

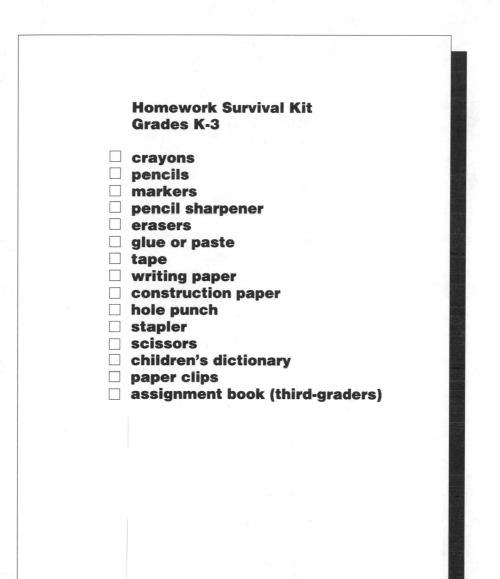

**Homework Survival Kit
Grades K-3**

- ☐ **crayons**
- ☐ **pencils**
- ☐ **markers**
- ☐ **pencil sharpener**
- ☐ **erasers**
- ☐ **glue or paste**
- ☐ **tape**
- ☐ **writing paper**
- ☐ **construction paper**
- ☐ **hole punch**
- ☐ **stapler**
- ☐ **scissors**
- ☐ **children's dictionary**
- ☐ **paper clips**
- ☐ **assignment book (third-graders)**

**Homework Survival Kit
Grades 4-6**

- [ ] pencils
- [ ] pens
- [ ] colored pencils
- [ ] crayons
- [ ] markers
- [ ] pencil sharpener
- [ ] erasers
- [ ] glue or paste
- [ ] tape
- [ ] writing paper
- [ ] construction paper
- [ ] hole punch
- [ ] stapler
- [ ] scissors
- [ ] paper clips
- [ ] white out
- [ ] assignment book
- [ ] folders for reports
- [ ] index cards
- [ ] intermediate dictionary
- [ ] atlas
- [ ] thesaurus
- [ ] almanac
- [ ] rubber bands

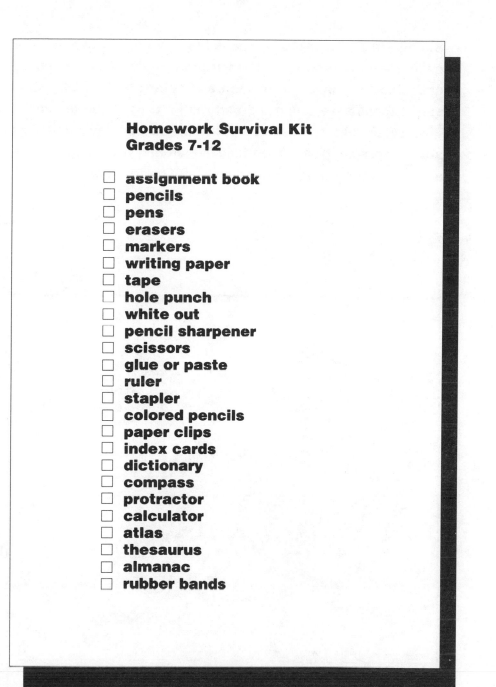

**Homework Survival Kit
Grades 7-12**

- ☐ **assignment book**
- ☐ **pencils**
- ☐ **pens**
- ☐ **erasers**
- ☐ **markers**
- ☐ **writing paper**
- ☐ **tape**
- ☐ **hole punch**
- ☐ **white out**
- ☐ **pencil sharpener**
- ☐ **scissors**
- ☐ **glue or paste**
- ☐ **ruler**
- ☐ **stapler**
- ☐ **colored pencils**
- ☐ **paper clips**
- ☐ **index cards**
- ☐ **dictionary**
- ☐ **compass**
- ☐ **protractor**
- ☐ **calculator**
- ☐ **atlas**
- ☐ **thesaurus**
- ☐ **almanac**
- ☐ **rubber bands**

Setting up a proper study area is the first step in getting your children—of any age—to do their homework successfully. By choosing an appropriate location, and by insisting that all necessary supplies are organized and ready to use, you are really giving your children a head start on homework achievement. This advance preparation is important. Remember, you are setting the stage for a long-running and successful performance!

HOMEWORK MUST BE DONE ON TIME

Homework Must Be Done on Time

There is probably no issue relating to homework that causes more parent-child conflict than when homework will be done each night. Children often argue about when they will do their homework. They try to put it off as long as possible. They complain, procrastinate, and make excuses until bedtime. Meanwhile, their parents are pushing them to do it as quickly as possible. In many homes, the issue of when homework will be done is the cause of nightly battles between parents and children. But it doesn't have to be that way. It shouldn't be that way. With a little bit of planning you can end this problem forever!

Think about this for a moment: Most children today have extremely busy — even complicated — agendas. They attend music lessons, sports events, and many other extracurricular activities frequently — sometimes on a daily basis. And yet they manage to attend these activities regularly, and on time. If gymnastics class begins at 4:00, that's when the child is there. That's because these activities are scheduled. They are built into the child's daily routine.

The solution to doing homework on time is clear:

Homework must be scheduled into your children's life, too.

It cannot be left up to your children to decide each night when homework will be done. Children cannot do homework effectively late at night. Children cannot regard homework as something to be done after all other activities have been attended to. Homework must be a priority. Homework must have a definite place in your children's schedule. Your involvement means that you must see that homework is done appropriately every day. You can do this by instituting Daily Homework Time in your home.

WHAT IS DAILY HOMEWORK TIME?

Daily Homework Time is a pre-planned time set aside each day during which your children must do homework. During Daily Homework Time all other activities must cease. Your children must understand that they are to stop playing, get off the phone, turn off the TV, go to their study areas and get to work. You and your children will agree in advance about when Daily Homework Time will be scheduled each day. The actual time chosen is unimportant. What is important is that you and your children will know each day when homework is expected to be done. Your children must understand that homework is their number-one priority. Setting up Daily Homework Time may be the single most important step you take in getting your children to do homework.

HOW TO SET UP DAILY HOMEWORK TIME

Tell your children exactly how you expect homework time to be scheduled.

"We want to help you schedule a time each day when you will do your homework. We want to make sure that you have a specific time to start your homework so that there is no question as to when you should do it. We also want to make sure that you allow enough time to do it well."

Make sure that all of your children's scheduled activities are written down on the Daily Schedule.

Make copies of the Daily Schedule on page 142 for each child. The Daily Schedule will help organize your children's time. By filling in all

DAILY SCHEDULE

MONDAY / HOMEWORK TIME:

3:00 PM	Soccer practice	7:00 PM	
4:00 PM	Soccer practice	8:00 PM	
5:00 PM		9:00 PM	Clarinet practice
6:00 PM		10:00 PM	

TUESDAY / HOMEWORK TIME:

3:00 PM	Clarinet practice	7:00 PM	Play rehearsal
4:00 PM	Scouts meeting	8:00 PM	
5:00 PM	Scouts meeting	9:00 PM	
6:00 PM		10:00 PM	

WEDNESDAY / HOMEWORK TIME:

3:00 PM	Dentist	7:00 PM	
4:00 PM	Clarinet practice	8:00 PM	
5:00 PM	dinner at Grandma's	9:00 PM	
6:00 PM		10:00 PM	

THURSDAY / HOMEWORK TIME:

3:00 PM		7:00 PM	
4:00 PM		8:00 PM	Clarinet practice
5:00 PM	Swim Team	9:00 PM	
6:00 PM	Swim Team	10:00 PM	

FRIDAY / HOMEWORK TIME:

3:00 PM		7:00 PM	
4:00 PM		8:00 PM	
5:00 PM		9:00 PM	
6:00 PM		10:00 PM	

scheduled activities for a given week, you and your children can clearly see what time is available for homework.

Follow these guidelines for completing the Daily Schedule:	
Grades K-3	Fill in the Daily Schedule with your child. Be sure to share the information, letting your child see how her activities fit into her day.
Grades 4-6	Have your child fill in the Daily Schedule by herself. Check it for accuracy.
Grades 7-12	Give your child a copy of the Daily Schedule to fill out on her own.

Determine the length of time needed each day for homework.

Homework time may range from fifteen minutes for younger children to two or more hours for high-school students.

Determine the best time period each day to be set aside for Daily Homework Time.

After you have blocked out all scheduled time on the Daily Schedule, consider all non-scheduled hours as eligible to be used for Daily Homework Time. Write down the Daily Homework Time for each night of the week in the designated space on the Daily Schedule.

DAILY SCHEDULE

MONDAY / HOMEWORK TIME: 7:00 – 8:30
3:00 PM Soccer practice	7:00 PM Homework
4:00 PM Soccer practice	8:00 PM
5:00 PM	9:00 PM Clarinet practice
6:00 PM	10:00 PM

TUESDAY / HOMEWORK TIME: 8:30 – 10:00
3:00 PM Clarinet practice	7:00 PM Play rehearsal
4:00 PM Scouts meeting	8:00 PM Homework 8:30
5:00 PM Scouts meeting	9:00 PM
6:00 PM	10:00 PM

WEDNESDAY / HOMEWORK TIME: 7:00 – 8:30
3:00 PM Dentist	7:00 PM Homework
4:00 PM Clarinet practice	8:00 PM
5:00 PM dinner at Grandma's	9:00 PM
6:00 PM	10:00 PM

THURSDAY / HOMEWORK TIME: 3:00 – 4:30
3:00 PM Homework	7:00 PM
4:00 PM	8:00 PM Clarinet practice
5:00 PM Swim Team	9:00 PM
6:00 PM Swim Team	10:00 PM

FRIDAY / HOMEWORK TIME: No Homework
3:00 PM	7:00 PM
4:00 PM	8:00 PM
5:00 PM	9:00 PM
6:00 PM	10:00 PM

Follow these guidelines for choosing Daily Homework Time:

Grades K-3   It is your responsibility to choose Daily Homework Time for your child.

Select a time when you or another responsible adult will be available to assist your child.

Try to schedule the same Daily Homework Time for all of your younger children. (This will make it more convenient for you to be available.)

Write down the homework hours in the designated spaces on the Daily Schedule.

Go over the sheet with your child, explaining what it means.

Post the sheet in a prominent location so that both you and your child will know exactly when homework will be done each day.

Grades 4-6   Have your child determine her own homework hours and write them in the designated spaces on the Daily Schedule.

Check the sheet to make sure that the homework times chosen are appropriate. (Does Daily Homework Time conflict with other scheduled activities? Is it scheduled for too late in the evening?)

Post the Daily Schedule in a prominent location so that both you and your child will know exactly when homework will be done each day.

Grades 7-12   It is your child's responsibility to determine her own homework hours, using the already completed Daily Schedule as a guide.

The preceding chart is meant to be a general guide. If your child is, for example, in the eighth grade, and having a lot of trouble with homework, you must back up and follow the suggestions given here for younger students. For a while, fill in the Daily Schedule (and choose Daily Homework Time) with your child. When homework improves, you may move ahead and allow your child to plan her schedule independently.

There may be days when your children complete all homework assignments before Daily Homework Time is over. If the work was done appropriately, your children should be allowed to proceed to other activities.

IF NECESSARY, ESTABLISH MANDATORY HOMEWORK TIME

The concept of Daily Homework Time can be altered to help you deal with two common types of homework problems. We call them "speeders" and "forgetters."

Speeders are children who race through their homework during Daily Homework Time with little or no effort. They want to "get it done" and get back to more pleasurable activities as quickly as possible. As a result, their homework is messy, incomplete, or incorrectly done.

Forgetters frequently fail to remember to bring work home, or "forget" that they have homework at all.

You can help speeders and forgetters become more responsible by instituting Mandatory Homework Time. Mandatory Homework Time means that children must use their entire scheduled Daily Homework Time for homework or other academic activities such as reading, reviewing textbooks, or practicing math.

The purpose of Mandatory Homework Time is to teach your children that there is no advantage to rushing through work or forgetting it altogether. It's not going to buy them any more free time. When children learn that their irresponsible approach to homework will not be rewarded with more free time, they will learn quickly to slow down and do a better job. They will suddenly start "remembering" that they do have homework, after all.

Here's how Mandatory Homework Time works:

Sit down with your child and tell her that some changes are going to be made:

"We are not happy with the way you rush through your homework. We're going to put some new rules into effect."

(or)

"We are not happy with your habit of forgetting to bring your homework home night after night. We're going to put some new rules into effect."

(continue with)

"You have one hour set aside for homework each night. You have not been using that time appropriately. If you speed through your homework (or forget your homework), you will still be expected to do academic work for the rest of the hour. You can read, study for tests, or brush up on classwork. You will not spend the time watching TV, playing computer games, or doing anything unrelated to school."

WHAT IF YOU CAN'T BE HOME DURING DAILY HOMEWORK TIME?

What do you do if you or your spouse's schedules do not permit either of you to be home during Daily Homework Time? It involves some additional planning and long-distance supervision, but it can be done.

Follow these guidelines if you can't be home during Daily Homework Time:

Grades K-3 As we mentioned before, young children must have someone available to help them when they do homework. Make sure that the person who supervises your children understands what Daily Homework Time means and will be available to give your child any help needed. If the caretaker cannot do this, it would be best to schedule your child's Daily Homework Time when you can be home.

Grades 4-6 Make sure that your child knows each day when Daily Homework Time begins. Telephone home at the start of Daily Homework Time to check to see that your child is working. Have her leave her homework out for you to review when you get home.

Grades 7-12 Your child should be able to do her homework unsupervised. Her grades and feedback from school will let you know whether or not homework is being done appropriately.

ENCOURAGE OLDER STUDENTS TO USE A WEEKLY PLANNER

In upper grades students are often given homework assignments for the entire week on Monday. Unless they record these assignments in an organized—and accurate—manner, they can easily run into trouble. Using a Weekly Planner can help your children in two ways:

By writing down all assignments and due dates for the week, your child can distribute the work so that everything is done on time—and not at the last minute.

Getting homework done correctly begins with writing the assignment down accurately when it is given. All too often children do less than their best on homework because they don't have correct or complete information.

This problem can be solved if your child learns to take a little more care in writing down assignments. Below you will see examples of two filled-in Weekly Planners. One has been done carefully, so that all pertinent information is written down. The other is incomplete and confusing. It is clear from these examples that one student stands a much better chance of doing her homework correctly than the other student.

Give your child a copy of the Weekly Planner (page 143 of the Appendix). Tell her that you expect her to use the Planner to record all homework assignments for the week. Show her the examples below and make sure she understands why writing down assignments accurately is so important.

WEEKLY PLANNER

NAME_____ DATE_____

SUBJECTS	MONDAY	TUESDAY	WEDNESDAY	THURSDAY	FRIDAY
Math	Pages 101-102	Test Friday	Page 111		
Social Studies	current events article	Questions p. 64	Quiz Fri		Quiz
English	Story about Pet.	Quiz Thurs.			
Science	Do experiment for Wed.	Read pages 140-150			

Incorrect: The information written down is incomplete.

WEEKLY PLANNER

NAME_____ DATE_____

SUBJECTS	MONDAY	TUESDAY	WEDNESDAY	THURSDAY	FRIDAY
Math	Pg. 101 #1-12 Pg. 102 #1-4 only	Test Fri. Study Chapter 14 – pages 99-112 only	pg. 111 Even problems. Show work. Study for test	Study for test pp 99-112 Review last quiz.	Test ✱
Social Studies	Get current events article for Thurs. Must be on S. America – from newspaper.	Answer questions 1-12 on p. 64 Use pen.	Quiz on Fri. Chapters 4-5. Study questions at end of chapters	Current events article due. Study for test	Quiz ✱
English	Creative Writing "My Favorite Pet" 2 pages. Rough draft due Thurs.	Quiz Thurs. (pp. 44-46) Work on story.	study for quiz Finish rough draft.	Quiz ✱ Turn in rough draft.	Final draft of "My Favorite Pet" due next Wed.
Science	Prepare an experiment from list on p. 147. Bring Wed.	Bring experiment tomorrow — Read pages 140-150. Answer questions on 150.	Experiment due. Present to whole class Fri.	Prepare notes for presentation of experiment.	Present Experiment to class.

Correct: All pertinent information has been written down.

Establishing Daily Homework Time may be the single most important step you take in solving your children's homework problems. No longer will homework be regarded as something to be "squeezed in" between other activities . . . if there's time. Daily Homework Time takes the guesswork — and the tears — out of getting homework done on time. When you establish Daily Homework Time, you are giving your children the message that homework is a number-one priority in your home.

Homework Without Tears Checklist

Let's see how you're doing.

Have you:

☐ Set up a proper study area in your home?

☐ Established Daily Homework Time?

CHILDREN MUST DO HOMEWORK ON THEIR OWN

Chapter 4

Children Must Do Homework on Their Own

As we discussed in Chapter 1, homework teaches children responsibility. Studies show that through homework, children learn skills that they must develop if they are to grow to be independent, motivated and successful adults. They learn to follow directions, begin and complete a task, and manage their time. It is, therefore, important that your children learn to do their homework on their own. But what do you do when your child comes to you, assignment in hand, and tells you, "I can't do this!"?

Some children complain continually that their homework is "too hard." It is often difficult to determine whether they really can't do it or whether they just don't want to do it. It may even be that the teacher has not adequately explained the assignment.

If your child has the ability to do the work, it may be that he simply lacks confidence and needs encouragement. It's a natural reaction for a parent to want to step in and help a child who seems to feel so helpless and inadequate. You feel terrible when your child comes to you dejectedly, holding his homework and saying, "I just don't understand it! I can't do it! I can't do anything!" He's feeling so overwhelmed that you step in and "help" by doing the homework for him.

In reality, you're not helping at all. By doing the work for him, you're confirming his belief that he is not capable of doing the work on his own. You are sending him a message that will result in his feeling even more overwhelmed the next time he has homework to do. The best help you can give your child is to encourage him to do the homework on his own.

HOW TO GET YOUR CHILDREN TO WORK ON THEIR OWN

Tell your children that you expect them to do homework on their own.

"We know that sometimes homework is difficult for you, but you are going to have to do your homework on your own. We (I) will not do your homework for you. We will be around to help you. But before you ask us for help, we expect you to try to solve the problem or answer the question—whatever it may be—on your own."

Your goal as a parent is for your children to do their homework independently. But this doesn't happen overnight. Working independently is a skill that must be nurtured and encouraged from the time your children first begin to receive homework assignments. That's why it's so important to start off right. Your increased involvement in encouraging your children to work alone when they are young will result in responsible, more independent older children.

Follow these guidelines for parental involvement:

Grades K-3   Check each day to see if your child has a homework assignment.

Tell your child when Daily Homework Time begins.

Check to see that your child has all necessary materials.

Ask your child to tell you what the homework assignment is.

If needed, read the directions together with your child. Make sure he understands what is expected.

If needed, get your child started by working on the first problem or question together.

Be available to answer questions and give assistance.

Praise your child's efforts. (See Chapter 5.)

Grades 4-6	Check to see that your child is doing homework at the proper time.
	Suggest that your child call a friend if he needs help.
	Give your child help only after he makes an effort on his own.
	Utilize study skills to help your child work independently. (See Chapter 11.)
	Praise your child's efforts. (See Chapter 5.)
Grades 7-12	Other than occasional exceptions, your child should be working independently. If he is having a great deal of trouble doing so, you must back up and follow the suggestions given here for younger students. The key is to start off with considerable involvement, then to reduce it gradually.
	Utilize study skills to help your child work more efficiently. (See Chapter 11.)

CAUTION!   Do not do the work for your children!
Do not teach concepts to your children!

Each day your children should carefully list all the homework that must be completed during Daily Homework Time. You may wish to check off each assignment as it is completed. It is helpful to have your children start with their least favorite subjects to make sure that their minds are fresh when dealing with these subjects.

Keep in mind that all children are different. Your child might be in the third grade and already working independently and responsibly. In this case, you don't need to sit down with him each night as he begins his homework. On the other hand, you might have a fifth-grader who still can't get down to business. If that's the situation, you need to back up a little. Guide him through the homework sequence of Grades K-3. When he's working independently, you can reduce your involvement.

Use the process of encouragement.

To encourage your children to work independently, it is necessary that you learn what we call the process of encouragement. It is a simple process that will enable you to build your children's confidence in their ability to do their homework on their own. Just keep these ideas in mind when your children continually ask for your help with assignments:

Emphasize your confidence in your children's ability to do the work with a little boost from you:

CHILD: I just don't know what to do. This page is too confusing.

PARENT: I know you think it's too hard, but I'm sure that with just a little help from me you'll be able to do it. Let's get started.

Break down the "overwhelming" assignment into simple steps you know your child can do successfully.

A child who feels inadequate may look at an assignment and not know where to begin. Help him divide it into easily managed steps. For example, have him begin simply by reading the instructions on a worksheet:

CHILD: I can't do this worksheet. It's too hard.

PARENT: Let's start with the directions at the top of the page. Please read them to me.

CHILD: "Draw a line under each word or phrase that has to do with the Revolutionary War."

Provide encouragement each time the child succeeds at any step. Then have him move forward to complete the assignment.

PARENT: Good. You can read the instructions. Do you know what they mean?

CHILD: Sure, underline the words that have to do with the Revolutionary War.

PARENT: Good. Now, do you know what the Revolutionary War means?

CHILD: Sure. We're studying it in school. That was the war against England when we won our independence.

PARENT: Great! Now let's try one of the words.

CHILD: "Valley Forge." That has to do with the Revolutionary War. I remember that one. I'll underline it.

PARENT: Good. You know that one. Try the next.

CHILD: "Slavery." No, I don't think that had anything to do with the Revolutionary War.

PARENT: Then do you want to underline it?

CHILD: No. Let's do the next one. "Musket." I don't know what that is. What's a musket?

PARENT: How can you find out what a musket is?

CHILD: You mean a dictionary? Oh, come on. Can't you just tell me?

PARENT: I know you know how to use a dictionary. Tell me when you find the definition.

Once your child begins gaining confidence, have him do a small part of the assignment on his own.

After each part is done, have him do the next part:

PARENT: You're doing great! Why don't you do the next ten words on your own? When you're finished, let me see your work.

(Ten minutes later)

PARENT: Hey, you got them all correct! Now I'll bet you can do the rest on your own!

It's often tempting to just go ahead and give your children the answer to a homework problem. It takes time to go through the process outlined on the past few pages. But keep in mind that you are doing much more than helping them through one assignment. By encouraging your children — step by step — to work on their own, you are helping them to develop greater confidence. And looking at it realistically, you simply can't continue indefinitely to do your children's homework for them. Eventually it will become too difficult even for you. How much algebra, Spanish, or chemistry do you remember?

Homework Without Tears Checklist

Have you:

 Set up a proper study area in your home?

Established Daily Homework Time?

Taken steps to encourage your children to do their homework independently?

MOTIVATE YOUR CHILDREN TO DO THEIR BEST WORK

Part One: Praise

Chapter 5

Motivate Your Children to Do Their Best Work
Part One: Praise

As a parent, you have a tremendous influence on your children's sense of self-esteem. What you say (or don't say) can make a big difference in how your children feel about themselves and about everything they do. Don't ever underestimate the power of your words or your actions!

Many children who lack the motivation to do homework don't feel secure in their ability to succeed in anything relating to school. They need encouragement and support from the people whose opinions they value most—their parents.

Without meaning to, you may be breaking down your children's confidence by some of the things you say and do. Do you tend to focus on their negative behavior? When children don't "shine" the way parents feel they ought to, it's dangerously easy to become frustrated, and respond to their lack of motivation with such comments as:

> "You just can't do your homework without messing up, can you?"

> "What's wrong with you? Can't you ever get moving without my having to hassle you?"

> "Is this your homework paper? It looks like chicken scratches!"

> "What's the matter with you? Don't you ever want to amount to anything?"

. . .And of course, the all-time resentment causer:

> "Why can't you do a good job like your sister does?"

No matter how frustrating your children's attitude might be for you, comments such as these only serve to erode their motivation and self-confidence. Always keep in mind that your continual positive support can and will motivate your children. The more your children are encouraged to feel good about their ability, the more motivated they will be to succeed.

HOW TO MOTIVATE YOUR CHILDREN WITH PRAISE

Consistently praise your children's efforts.

The secret to motivating your children through praise is to be consistent. Don't save your praise only for an "A" on a test. Praise your children for their efforts each day. It is, after all, the day-to-day efforts that will lead to higher achievement in school—and to those good grades. Let your children know that you appreciate just how hard they are trying!

> "You really tried hard on this assignment! Good job!"

> "I'm delighted about the way you're starting your homework on time every day!"

> "Eight out of ten spelling words correct! That's a big improvement over last time. It shows how hard you're trying!"

> "I really like how you're doing your homework on your own now. Good job!"

> "I think it's great that you're working straight through Daily Homework Time and even a little longer when you have to. I'm really proud of you!"

Tell your children specifically what you like about what they are doing or what they have done.

> "I really do appreciate your doing your homework without arguing" sounds more sincere and has a much greater effect on your children's self-esteem than "You're doing a good job." It shows that you really are noticing exactly what your children are accomplishing.

Praise is important to children of all ages. **Follow these guidelines for giving praise:**	
Grades K-3	With young children it's important to praise all homework efforts. Let your child know just how proud you are of how hard she is working. Find lots of specific things each night to praise your child about.
Grades 4-6	Each night praise your child about some specific accomplishment.
Grades 7-12	Older children need praise too. Make sure that at least once a week you praise your child about a specific accomplishment. (Ask to see a homework assignment.)

Remember that a hug or a pat on the shoulder will increase the impact of your message.

The key to motivating your children is letting them know how much you care about them and the effort they are making. A hug or a pat on the shoulder will strengthen your message.

Use Super Praise to motivate your children.

A powerful tool for letting your children feel your appreciation for their efforts is a technique we call Super Praise. Here's how to use it:

First, one parent praises the child for her behavior: "I really appreciate how hard you're working to do your homework. You finished it all during Daily Homework Time and you did a great job. I want to make sure Dad hears about this when he gets home."

Second, this parent praises the child in front of the other parent: "Patty did a really fine job on her homework today. She started it without complaining, she stayed with it, and she did just a super job on it."

Finally, the other parent praises the child: "I really felt proud of you, getting such a good report from Mom. You're really doing fine!"

If you're a single parent, you can use a grandparent, a neighbor, or a family friend as your partner in delivering Super Praise. Any adult whose approval your children will value can fill the role of the second person offering praise.

Praise is appreciated by all children. It is particularly important for children who are hard to motivate. Keep in mind the enormous impact your praise can have on building their self-esteem and on helping them to develop appropriate behavior concerning homework. With your continual positive support, children can be motivated to develop a positive self-image and to approach homework with a confident, I-can-do-it attitude.

Homework Without Tears Checklist

Have you:

 Set up a proper study area in your home?

Established Daily Homework Time?

Taken steps to encourage your children to do their homework independently?

Consistently praised your children's efforts?

MOTIVATE YOUR CHILDREN TO DO THEIR BEST WORK

Part Two:
Great Ideas That Really Work!

Motivate Your Children to Do Their Best Work
Part Two: Great Ideas That Really Work!

Some children would attempt to walk on water merely to receive their parents' praise. For these children, consistent praise is enough to stimulate and to sustain enthusiasm about homework. But other children are more difficult to motivate with words alone. With these children, you have to use additional incentives.

You may think that your children should be motivated to do homework without receiving something in return. The idea of "paying off" your children for doing what is expected may make you uncomfortable. But keep in mind that everyone needs and wants encouragement and praise for the work they do. Most of the time, a simple pat on the back is enough. But there are times when something more is needed. An incentive is simply something that motivates one to action. If this added incentive is what it takes to get your children motivated to do their homework, then by all means try it. Once they are working on their own you will be able to "phase out" the "rewards" and keep them motivated by your praise.

Note: It is important to remember that offering incentives is appropriate *only* after a considerable amount of praise has failed to motivate your children to do their homework appropriately.

HOW TO MOTIVATE YOUR CHILDREN TO DO THEIR BEST WORK

Tell your children that you are going to use some new ideas to help them do their homework.

"We know that doing homework is hard at times. We have some great ideas that will make it more enjoyable for you. When you do your work appropriately, you will earn a reward. We're doing this because we really want to help you want to do your best!"

Choose an incentive that your child will appreciate.

Ask yourself, "What sort of motivation will work best with my child?"
The incentive should not strain your budget or your time schedule, but
it should be something that is meaningful to the child. Some children
will be motivated by staying up late or by sharing activities with you.
Others would groan at the thought of spending more time in family
activities, but might appreciate baseball cards, a trip to a video
arcade, or an afternoon with a special friend. Don't try to motivate your
child with something he doesn't care about.

> "Kevin, you did such a good job starting your homework
> without arguing that you can stay up 15 minutes later
> tonight."

> "Gail, you've been bringing your homework home and
> doing it by yourself so responsibly this week! Let's go to
> lunch on Saturday."

> "Jeff, you did all your homework this week. You can go
> to the party on Saturday night."

Be consistent.

Giving incentives once or twice will not produce results. Be prepared
to reward your children consistently for several days, a week or two,
or even longer, depending on their behavior and response. You might
choose to use an incentive or privilege once or twice a week, backed
up by praise on the other days. Remember, though, only consistent
motivation will produce results.

Phase out incentives.

Don't worry. You aren't expected to give your children incentives indefinitely. Once they have demonstrated that they can do their
homework appropriately you can begin to phase out the incentives.
(In nearly all cases, children will by then have become conditioned to
do their homework responsibly.) But be sure that you continue to give
your children plenty of verbal praise. That's something that they will
always need and want plenty of!

Remember that giving incentives is *your* choice.

There are children who may become conditioned to doing their homework in exchange for an incentive: "I won't do it unless you let me stay up later." "I will not do my book report unless you give me a prize."

If this happens, lay down the law at once. Do not allow your children to involve you in a power struggle. Do not allow them to extort incentives from you. Set firm limits the very first time they exhibit any threatening behavior. Let them know it will not be tolerated:

> "Janey, doing your homework on your own is your job. Offering you a reward for doing it is my choice. Don't ever get the idea that it's something you have coming to you."

GREAT MOTIVATING IDEAS

The following pages contain a variety of games and other motivational ideas. All of these ideas have been used successfully by parents to make homework a more positive experience for even the most difficult children. Use the chart below as a guideline for deciding which motivators might work best for your children. But remember, this is only a guideline. You know your children best. Use whatever motivators you feel will work with them.

Grades K-3	Beat the Clock Spinner Homework Award Homework Contract
Grades 4-6	Trade Off Chunking Spinner Homework Award Homework Contract
Grades 7-12	Homework Contract

Beat the Clock

Use this game with children who seem to take forever to do their homework.

Determine how long it should take your child to finish his homework assignment. Then, at the start of Daily Homework Time, tell him you have a new, fun way to help him get through his work:

1. "You'll have an hour (or a half hour, or whatever time you determine) to get tonight's assignment finished.

2. I'm going to set this oven timer (stopwatch, etc.) for 60 minutes. If you get your homework done correctly before the timer goes off, then you'll get . . .(whatever reward you've chosen)."

You may want to use this game in conjunction with the Homework Contract on page 146.

1. Make a copy of the Homework Contract. Post the contract on the refrigerator or in another prominent location.

2. Instead of offering a reward each time your child "beats the clock," offer him a sticker.

3. When the child has accumulated five stickers (or three or ten, etc.), he gets a prize.

Phasing Out: The number of stickers needed to earn a reward should increase as the child becomes more responsible about his homework.

Spinner

This fun and motivational technique can be used successfully to develop your children's enthusiasm about homework.

You will need one game spinner to do this activity. (Spinners can be found in educational supply stores or check inside old boxed games that are not played with anymore.)

1. Place a plain white adhesive label on each of the sections of the spinner. Fill in each section with a reward or a privilege your child would like (see Illustration A for ideas). Use a pencil so that you can occasionally change the awards offered. Be sure to vary the prizes on the spinner. Some should be more desirable than others. You may even want to have a space marked NO WIN.

2. Tell your child: "Each time you do your homework appropriately you will earn a spin on the spinner. You will win whatever reward the spinner points to."

If you use the spinner, use it consistently. Each time your child does his homework according to the rules, tell him, "Great job on your homework tonight; you've earned a spin on the spinner."

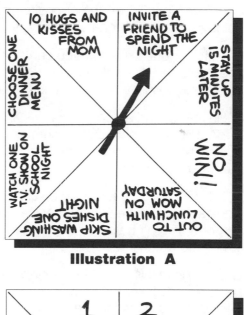

Illustration A

Phasing Out: Mark the spaces on the spinner with numbers indicating points (see Illustration B). Tell your child that the points will count toward a prize. (For example, when a child has earned 10 points he wins a specified prize.) Increase the number of points needed to earn a reward as your child becomes more responsible about homework.

Illustration B

Trade Off!

This is a game for younger children who can't seem to develop the self-confidence to do their homework independently, no matter how often you give encouragement.

Some children continue to be afraid of working without you right there holding their hand, while others keep interrupting you with unnecessary questions every time they do their homework. With these children, stopping all assistance at once and refusing to help can cause stress and conflict — the opposite effect of the one you're trying to achieve. Trade Off! can gradually reduce their need for your help.

1. Tell your child: "I know you can do your homework on your own. I know you can do it without asking me so many questions. Let's play a game that will help you do this."

2. Have on hand a supply of some small item that your child will appreciate and that you feel comfortable in giving him: peanuts, raisins, M & Ms or other small candies. Place ten of them in a bowl at the child's study area.

3. Tell your child: "Each time you ask me for help with your homework, you have to give me one of these candies (raisins, etc.). When they're all gone, I won't help you any more. At the end of Daily Homework Time, you get to keep what's left."

Children love this game. In addition to wanting to keep as many of the items as possible, they have the added incentive of winning. When asking you a question means giving up something he wants, your child will think twice about it and try to come up with the answer on his own.

Phasing Out: Gradually decrease the number of items you start with each time you initiate the game. If you start with ten peanuts, reduce the number to eight after the first few times you play. Reduce the number several more times before phasing out the game. Or use the same number but increase the duration of the game. Instead of giving him a new supply of peanuts each time he has homework to do, tell him he must make it last for three days, then for a week.

As you gradually reduce the number of questions he can ask, you condition him to work independently in a fun, non-threatening manner.

Chunking

This is a great technique to use when your children's homework assignment seems just too much to do!

Sometimes young children have a difficult time with a homework assignment simply because it overwhelms them. They look an assignment of, say, 40 math problems, and don't even want to begin. "Chunking" can make the job seem manageable. Simply put, "chunking" means dividing a big assignment into smaller chunks. For example, you might divide the 40 math problems into groups of five problems each. When your child finishes each group of five problems, he earns a small reward.

Tell your child: "This is a big homework assignment, but I know that you can do it all! Let's play a game that will make it easier. I've marked off the first five problems on your worksheet. I want you to do these problems on your own. When you've finished them, you will receive a prize! We'll keep working this way with every group of five problems until the whole assignment is done!"

Phasing Out: As your child becomes more comfortable with long assignments, break them down into fewer chunks (for example, 4 groups of 10 problems each, then 2 groups of 20 problems each). Instead of earning 8 small rewards, your child will earn 4, then 2, then 1.

Homework Contract

A Homework Contract is an effective motivator that can work well with children of any age. It is an especially valuable tool because it encourages children to accept responsibility for an agreement made between them and their parents.

A Homework Contract is an agreement between you and your child that states, "When you do your homework appropriately, you will earn a reward."

For example:

"Each day that you bring home your homework and complete it on your own during Daily Homework Time, you will earn one point. When you have earned five points, you may choose one night to stay up late."

or

"Each day you start your homework promptly without arguing about it, you earn one point. When you have earned ten points, we'll go out for lunch."

A contract is one of the best ways to structure the motivation you give your children. Follow the guidelines below when making and using a short-term Homework Contract with your child:

Design the contract so that your child can earn an appropriate reward in a reasonable length of time.

The younger the child, the more quickly he should be able to earn the reward. Use this table as a guide, taking into consideration the particular needs of your child.

Age of Child	Minimum Time Required to Earn Reward
Grades K-3	Three to five days
Grades 4-6	One to two weeks
Grades 7-12	Two to four weeks

Make copies of the Homework Contract on page 146 of the Appendix. Fill in the following information:

The number of points that must be earned to receive the reward.

What reward the child will earn when homework is completed appropriately.

For each point earned, the child makes a check in one of the boxes. When he has accumulated the agreed-upon number of checks, he gets the reward. Be sure to display the Homework Contract in a prominent location.

The contract should be in effect for a specific period of time: one or two weeks to a month or more. When the contract has expired, discuss with your child whether it will be helpful to draw up a new one. Ask your child whether he wants something different for the reward.

Phasing Out: As your child begins to do homework independently and responsibly you can increase the number of points it takes to earn the reward. In this way you condition him to appropriate behavior. (Change the point system when you draw up new contracts.)

Homework Awards

Applaud your children's efforts at homework by giving them award certificates they can display in their room, on the refrigerator, or on the family bulletin board. An award will let them know just how proud you are of the work they're doing. Awards for different age levels have been included on pages 144 and 145 of the Appendix.

HOMEWORK CONTRACT

- Each day that you complete all your homework assignments, check off one square.

- When you have checked off _10_ squares, you will earn a reward.

- Your reward will be _tickets to a ball game_

Sylvia Smith
PARENT'S SIGNATURE

Ryan Smith
STUDENT'S SIGNATURE

✓	✓	✓	✓	

Expiration Date _4/26_

HOORAY!

_____
(Name)
is doing a great job on homework!

Homework Super Star

Providing unmotivated children with the needed incentives to do homework can be a major step forward in getting homework done responsibly. Don't be afraid to try motivational ideas of your own. After all, you know your children better than anyone else does. If you have a game or other incentive you think just might do the trick, by all means, try it!

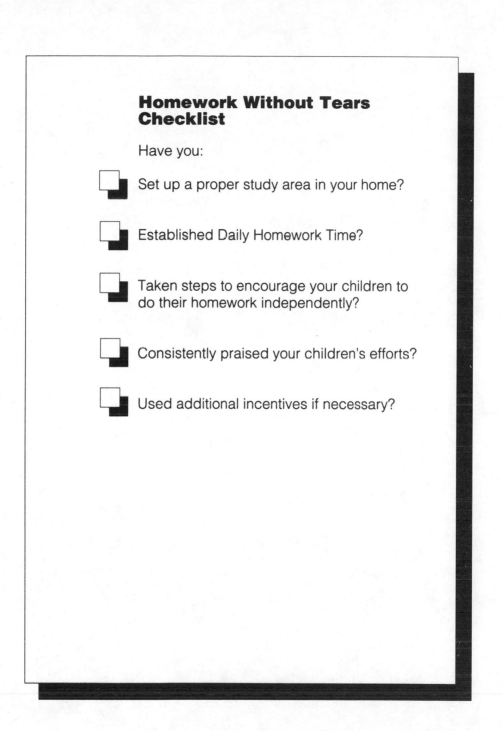

Homework Without Tears Checklist

Have you:

☐ Set up a proper study area in your home?

☐ Established Daily Homework Time?

☐ Taken steps to encourage your children to do their homework independently?

☐ Consistently praised your children's efforts?

☐ Used additional incentives if necessary?

IF YOUR CHILDREN ARE NOT DOING THEIR HOMEWORK

Communicate Assertively

If Your Children Are Not Doing Their Homework: Communicate Assertively

So now you've done it all. You've set up a quiet study area for your children. You've established the idea of a specific time each day when your children will do nothing but academic work. You've taken steps to ensure that they'll work on their own. You've provided your children with praise and motivational incentives. By now you must be sitting back and relaxing in your favorite chair each night while your children are keeping quietly busy with their homework. Your troubles are over! What's that? Your children are still arguing with you about their homework?

If that's the case, then it's time to look at how you're communicating with them throughout the homework process. Simply telling your children that you expect them to do homework may not be enough. Some children will put up an argument in an attempt to get out of doing the work. What happens next depends upon how you respond. You must learn to speak so that your children will listen: You must learn to communicate assertively.

When you communicate assertively you say what you mean and mean what you say. You give your children direct messages that leave no doubt in their mind what you want them to do. This way of speaking is critical when you want your children to really listen to you.

All too often parents resort to begging, pleading, or asking pointless questions when trying to get their children to behave appropriately:

> "Please, I can't take it any more. You've got to do your homework!"

> "How many times do I have to talk to you about doing your homework?"

> "What am I going to do with you? What does it take to get you to do your homework?"

Such statements do not clearly communicate what you want your children to do. They are vague, inexplicit, and ultimately ineffective. Likewise, making hostile statements, yelling and screaming are equally ineffective:

> "What's wrong with you? Can't you ever do anything the way you're supposed to?"

> "I'm sick of wasting my time trying to get you to do your homework."

> "You'd better shape up or you won't ever amount to anything!"

Such hostility is degrading to your children. It eats away at their self-confidence, contributing to the problem, not to the solution. It increases their resentment. When you yell and scream at your children, you communicate your anger and your ineffectiveness — not your authority; the message that homework must be completed does not even get through! Worse, all of these responses will teach your children not to listen to you at all.

Remember, you're in charge. You must create a position of firmness that will make even the most obstinate children think they've come up against a wall of resolve. You are the parent. You don't have to argue or plead with or yell at your children. You do have to firmly state your expectations. Homework must be done. You have to say what you mean and mean what you say.

HOW TO COMMUNICATE ASSERTIVELY

Tell your children — clearly and firmly — that you expect them to do their homework responsibly.

If your children are still arguing with you over homework in spite of all you've done, you must consider their attitude completely unacceptable. You've given them plenty of chances. Now they've got to understand that you mean what you say.

Sit down with each child individually. Look the child in the eye, and state your expectation in a calm, firm manner:

"In this home, your number-one responsibility is to do your homework. There will be no more arguments about it. You will do your homework on your own. You will do your homework during Daily Homework Time. And you will do it to the best of your ability."

Don't argue with your children. Use the Broken-Record technique.

As you are probably very aware, children often argue when parents ask them to do something they don't want to do. Unfortunately, we often argue back. This will not get results! Do not fall into the trap of arguing with your children:

PARENT: It's homework time!

CHILD: Just a few more minutes. I want to watch just one more program. Pleeeeze?

PARENT: You always want more time. Come on, it's time to do your homework.

CHILD: You're not fair. You never let me watch TV. You're always getting on my case.

PARENT: What do you mean, I'm on your case? I'm not on your case. All you ever do is watch TV.

CHILD: That's not true. You just like to pick on me. You never pick on Seth when he doesn't do his homework. You're not fair!

PARENT: I don't think I'm unfair . . .

This is all wrong. By arguing with the child, the parent has lost control of the situation. The focus has shifted from the child's responsibility to the parent's fairness. The child has succeeded in manipulating the parent and has evaded homework again or started an argument that has nothing to do with homework.

When your children argue with you about homework, simply repeat your expectation in a firm, clear manner. Use what we call the Broken-Record technique. Make yourself sound like a record that is stuck in a groove. Keep repeating what it is you want — "I want you to do your homework" — no matter what arguments your child puts up.

PARENT: It's homework time. I want you to start your homework now.

CHILD: Just a few more minutes. I just want to watch just one more program, pleeeze?

PARENT: (using Broken Record) I understand, but I want you to do your homework now.

CHILD: You're not fair. You never let me watch TV.

PARENT: (using Broken Record) I understand, but I want you to start your homework now.

CHILD: Okay, okay, I'll do it.

By using the Broken-Record technique, you avoid being sidetracked by the child's argument and you communicate to the child that you expect homework to be done. Here are some simple guidelines for using the Broken-Record technique when your child argues with you:

Determine what you want the child to do: "I want you to do your homework."

Keep repeating what you want when the child argues with you. Do not respond to any statement made by the child.

Use the Broken-Record technique a maximum of three times. If your child continues to argue and does not do homework, then you will need to follow through and "back up your words with action" as described in Chapter 8.

Arguing with your children is a no-win situation. The only result is that everyone gets angry, nothing is solved, and whatever message you're trying to communicate is lost. When you learn to speak so that your children listen, everybody feels better. You feel good because you've calmly stated your expectations, and your children feel better because they know exactly what's expected of them.

Homework Without Tears Checklist

Have you:

☐ Set up a proper study area in your home?

☐ Established Daily Homework Time?

☐ Taken steps to encourage your children to do their homework independently?

☐ Consistently praised your children's efforts?

☐ Used additional incentives if necessary?

☐ Communicated so that your children really listen?

Chapter 8

BACK UP YOUR WORDS WITH ACTION

"WE KNOW YOU'VE BEEN HAVING PROBLEMS WITH YOUR HOMEWORK SO WE'VE HIRED A SPECIAL HOMEWORK COUNSELOR TO GET YOU MOTIVATED."

Back Up Your Words with Action

Sometimes even the most carefully chosen words just aren't enough. No matter how you've tried to motivate with praise, no matter how assertively you've communicated, it just isn't working. Your child is still not doing his homework. Now you have to back up your words with action. It's time for you to communicate to your child, with full parental authority, that nothing else he does is to take precedence over homework.

First of all, look at your situation realistically. You can't make your child do his homework. You can't make him pick up a pen and write a report. You can't make him read a chapter in his textbook. Your child has to do that for himself. But you can do something:

Remember that homework teaches children that they are responsible for their own actions. If your child hasn't gotten the message by now, you're about to make it clearer. You're about to place the responsibility right where it belongs: squarely on your child's shoulders. You are going to give him a choice.

The choice is this: Your child assumes his responsibility to do his homework appropriately or else he chooses to have all privileges suspended until homework is finished. In other words, your child will choose to sit at his desk until his homework is finished. If that takes the entire night, it is his choice.

Do you see the difference? Instead of telling your child what to do, you are making him responsible for his actions—and their consequences. If your child chooses not to do homework, fine. He also chooses not to have privileges.

Many parents have great difficulty taking such a firm, assertive posture with their children. Some parents are afraid that they may harm their children psychologically if they come on too strong. Others are simply afraid that their children won't like them.

But such a stand must be taken. This is the reality of the situation. It is in our children's best interest. It is the only way they will ever learn to assume their responsibility when it comes to homework.

HOW TO BACK UP YOUR WORDS WITH ACTION

Tell your children that the choice is theirs.

Tell your children exactly what you mean:

"You have a choice. You can do your homework during Daily Homework Time or you can choose not to have privileges. If you choose not to do your homework, then from the beginning of Daily Homework Time until you have finished your homework you will lose these privileges: You will not leave this house. You will not watch TV. You will not listen to music. You will not be allowed to use the telephone, either to make or to receive calls. You will sit there until your homework is done. The choice is yours."

By clearly expressing your expectations, you leave no doubt about what you want your children to do and what the consequences will be if they fail to do it.

Don't make meaningless threats of punishment.

Vague threats that are not backed up with action communicate to your children that you don't mean what you say.

> "You're gonna do your homework—or else!"

> "I mean it! Next time you give me any hassle about homework, you're grounded for a month!"

"I'm not kidding! You'll be punished if you don't get to work!"

Be consistent in following through with your demands.

Consistency is the key to teaching your children that you mean business with homework as well as with other issues. Children must understand that you are not going to compromise—that you are not going to back down — that every night you will make sure that they assume the responsibility of doing homework.

Both you and the child must recognize that he may have to sit at his work area night after night, doing nothing but staring at the wall, until he chooses to do his homework responsibly:

CHILD: My favorite show is on. Let me watch it, please? I'll finish my homework at school. I promise.

PARENT: Justin, Daily Homework Time begins at 7:30. It's 8:00 now and you have not done your homework. You must finish your work before you do anything else.

CHILD: Just this one show, please? I haven't watched TV for three nights!

PARENT: That's because you chose not to work during Daily Homework Time the last three nights.

CHILD: I hate homework! It's boring!

PARENT: I understand, but the rule is that you must finish your homework before you can watch TV.

CHILD: This is gross. I'm never going to be able to watch TV again.

PARENT: Sure you will. When you choose to get down to business and do your homework during Daily Homework Time, you can watch TV after you're finished.

Be prepared for your children to test you to see if you mean business.

Many children will test their parents about the seriousness of their expectations regarding homework. There are several tactics they may use to challenge you.

Crying

When told that he cannot have any privileges until he finishes his homework, a child may cry or scream. Experience has taught him that this tactic will make his parents back down, either through guilt, or through aggravation. No matter how upset your child becomes, stand your ground calmly and follow through by insisting on your expectations:

CHILD: I'm tired of doing homework! I want to watch TV.

PARENT: (calmly) Terry, there will be no TV until your homework is finished.

CHILD: (starting to cry) I'll never finish this. I'll be doing homework all night long.

PARENT: (still calm) Terry, I understand how upset you are. But crying isn't going to help you get it done.

CHILD: (sobbing) You're terrible! You make me sit here and do this lousy homework!

PARENT: (still calm) Terry, you can cry if you like. But you're still going to have to do your homework. The longer you choose to cry, the longer it will take you to do it.

Anger

Your child may react with anger to your demands regarding homework. She is trying to use her anger to intimidate you into backing down. Do not let your child's anger affect you. Do not engage her in an argument. Remain calm, firm, and in control.

PARENT: Ellen, please get off the telephone. You know you aren't allowed to use the phone until homework is done.

CHILD: (angrily) Oh, come on! Just leave me alone!

PARENT: (staying calm) Ellen, I said you can't use the telephone until you finish your homework.

CHILD: (yelling) Why are you so mean? None of the other kids have to get off the phone while they do their homework!

PARENT: (calmly) That's not the point. You have to finish your homework before you can use the phone.

CHILD: (to friend on phone) I have to get off now. My parents are such a pain! I'll call you later.

Indifference

Some children seem to be willing to sit at their work spaces all night, night after night, acting as if they don't care. These children hope to manipulate parents into thinking that nothing can motivate them to do their homework. Eventually, your child hopes, you will give up trying. But he'll start caring when you follow through consistently with your demands.

PARENT: Derek, have you finished your homework?

CHILD: No, and I don't care if I have to sit here all night.

PARENT: (calmly) It's your choice, Derek, but I hope you change your mind sooner or later.

Whether your child's tactic is crying and screaming, hostility and cursing, an "I-don't-care" attitude, or a combination of all of them, don't let it dissuade you. Stand your ground. Let your child know that attempts at manipulating you will not work and that, in the end, your child will still have to do the homework.

If you can't be home during Daily Homework Time, monitor your children to make sure they are doing homework.

This conflict was previously discussed in Chapter 3. It's a problem that is encountered most frequently by single parents and by parents in dual-career families. But even in many "traditional" families, it is often not possible for either parent to be home to supervise their children during Daily Homework Time.

If your child is continuing to resist homework, this problem can be especially serious. You must make sure that the person providing child care in your absence is prepared to enforce the rules. You must leave specific instructions concerning your child's homework and what he is expected to do. Make sure that this person knows that during Daily Homework Time the child is to be doing nothing but homework, doing it at his work space, and doing it independently. If possible, call home during Daily Homework Time to check up on your child's progress. Tell him to be sure to leave his homework out where you can look at it when you get home.

Call the school if your children still will not do their homework.

Some children will choose to sit at their desk night after night and still not do their homework satisfactorily—even when they are quite capable of doing so. If this happens in your home, notify your child's teacher. Let the teacher know that your child did not complete the work and see if he or she can help.

With many children, it is helpful for you to establish the idea that you and the teacher are working together to make sure they do their homework. Making the teacher your partner in improving your children's homework performance is the subject of our next chapter.

Stand your ground with your children. They must understand that you will not argue, you will not fight, and that you will see that they do their homework . . .or else accept the consequences. You know how important it is to your children's future success that they start taking homework seriously and you're taking action to see that they do! Giving your children a choice makes them accept the responsibility for their own actions. Don't back down on your demands. And be sure to notify your children's teacher if homework problems continue.

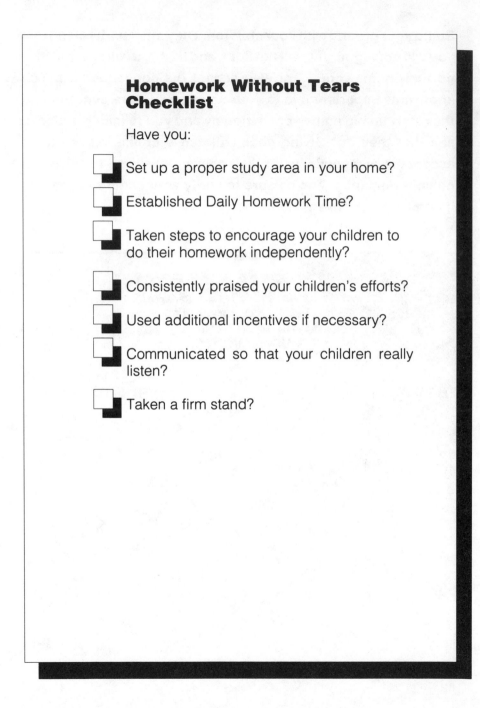

Homework Without Tears Checklist

Have you:

☐ Set up a proper study area in your home?

☐ Established Daily Homework Time?

☐ Taken steps to encourage your children to do their homework independently?

☐ Consistently praised your children's efforts?

☐ Used additional incentives if necessary?

☐ Communicated so that your children really listen?

☐ Taken a firm stand?

YOUR PARTNER AT SCHOOL —THE TEACHER

Your Partner at School —the Teacher

As we mentioned earlier, homework is the key link between home and school. There are times when your children's homework problems can be solved only by a coordinated effort between you and the teacher.

There are two guidelines to keep in mind concerning working with your children's teacher. First, do not hesitate to contact him when your children are having homework problems that you can't solve with the methods presented in *Homework Without Tears.* The sooner the teacher is alerted to the problem, the sooner action can be taken.

Second, do not be intimidated by the teacher. Many parents are reluctant to "bother" her, or are afraid to tell her anything about their children's problems. Good teachers want to know if children are having difficulties. They don't want to be left in the dark. They will invite your comments and welcome your sharing of information and ideas.

At the same time, don't make the mistake of considering any difficulties your children might be having as "the teacher's problem." The teacher has her function in your children's education, and you have yours. It's very easy to deny any responsibility for your children's academic success by saying, "It's the teacher's fault," or, "It's the school's fault." Instead of finding fault, consider what you and the teacher can do, as partners, to solve the problem and ensure your children's success. Be prepared to consider anything the teacher might tell you, even if it comes as an unpleasant surprise.

When you form a partnership with the teacher, you are letting your children know that home and school are putting up a united front to help them succeed. That's a powerful message that will bring results!

HOW AND WHEN TO CONTACT THE TEACHER

Contact the teacher if your child cannot do the homework assignments.

If your children encounter homework assignments that they cannot do, the teacher should know. Once again, resist any temptation you may have to step in and teach the child the concepts behind any homework assignment. Teaching is not your job. And once again, do not step in and do the assignment for your child.

Your first communication with the school should be a note to the teacher letting him know that your child isn't doing the assigned work. You may want to include your observations of what happens when the child tries to do the work. Is the problem with understanding ideas or with understanding how to apply them? If the problem continues, it's time to call the teacher to discuss the problem or set up a conference. The problem may have any of several causes. Your child may daydream in class; she may be encountering difficulties with a particular subject; she may have an undetected learning disability. The teacher may be giving out homework that covers concepts which the child has not yet mastered or that is otherwise inappropriate (if this is the case, most of the class will be having the same difficulty). A parent-teacher conference is often all that is necessary to pinpoint the source of the problem and to come up with a solution.

Contact the teacher if your child does not bring home assigned work.

When children continue to "forget" their homework or fail to bring it home, you must work with the teacher to correct the problem. Only by contacting the school can you find out what work your child should be doing. The best way to handle the problem is to require your child to bring home a homework log: a record of each day's assignments. See sample Homework Assignment Log sheets on pages 147 and 148 of the

HOMEWORK ASSIGNMENT LOG

NAME _____

DATE _____

PERIOD	CLASS	HOMEWORK ASSIGNMENT	TEACHER'S SIGNATURE
1			
2			
3			
4			
5			
6			

Appendix.) Ask your child's teacher(s) to write down all assignments in the log and to sign and date them for verification. If no homework is assigned on a particular day, ask the teacher to indicate "no assignment." Each day before Daily Homework Time begins, sit down with your child and go over the assignments in the log.

If your child "loses" the log, or "forgets" to bring it home, you have a situation that calls for Mandatory Homework Time as we discussed in Chapter 3.

Your child should be required to remain at her work space throughout Daily Homework Time, keeping busy at some form of academic work. Then, first thing the next morning, contact the teacher. Your child will see that you and the teacher are partners in making sure she does her homework responsibly.

Contact the teacher if your child does not finish homework assignments.

Each night your child does not complete her homework, send a note to the teacher indicating this has occurred, and that you hope the teacher will follow through at school. It may be necessary to have a conference with the teacher to iron out the details of this plan.

Contact the teacher if your child does a poor job on homework assignments or exhibits poor work habits.

Some children do muddle through their assigned work, but do an inadequate job. The work may be sloppy or full of errors. This may happen because the child has poor work habits, or because she just can't understand the material. A conference with the teacher can help you determine the cause of the problem and discuss possible solutions.

If your child has poor work habits, the teacher may ask you to take a more active role with homework. He may actually want you to correct the work and demand your child improve her work. Normally, you should not correct your child's homework. That's the teacher's job. But if the teacher asks you to correct her work, let your child know that the teacher expects better work habits and has asked you to help out.

WHAT IF YOUR CHILD IS BORED?

There is one factor we haven't discussed yet that may be causing your child's homework problems, at least in part. She may be "forgetting" to bring work home, failing to complete it, or doing a lackluster job on it simply because she is bored.

We all can sympathize with our children in such a situation. We all can remember dull, unimaginative teachers who could have left a budding Einstein disgusted with physics, or turned off a young Emily Dickinson to the English language forever. You may look at your child's homework assignments and think, "She's right, this is boring. It's utterly pointless!"

But that shouldn't matter. It's not the specifics of the work that we're concerned with. It's the process. Life can often seem like meaningless busywork. If your child is unlucky enough to be stuck with an uninspiring teacher, don't let her use this fact as an excuse to avoid doing homework. She must be kept aware that she is expected to complete all assignments, whether they're exciting, deadly dull, or somewhere in between.

Otherwise, you and the teacher will be working at cross-purposes. Instead of making the teacher your partner, you'll be inviting your child to play one of you against the other — while she avoids her responsibility to do homework.

Don't hesitate to form a partnership with the teacher. Let your children know that home and school are putting up a united front to help them succeed.

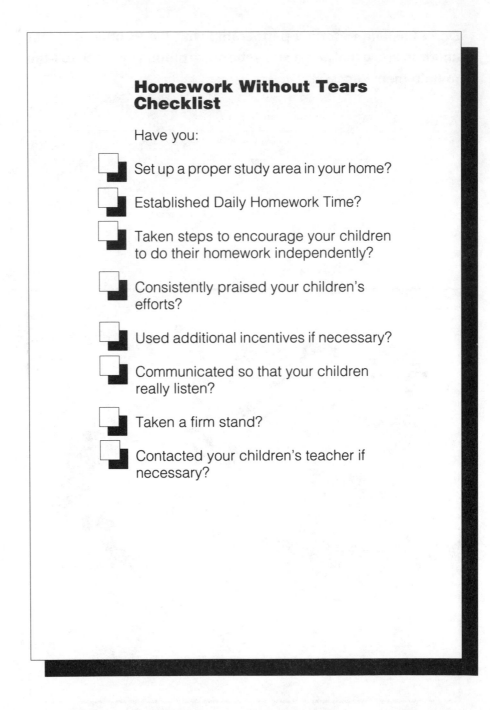

Homework Without Tears Checklist

Have you:

☐ Set up a proper study area in your home?

☐ Established Daily Homework Time?

☐ Taken steps to encourage your children to do their homework independently?

☐ Consistently praised your children's efforts?

☐ Used additional incentives if necessary?

☐ Communicated so that your children really listen?

☐ Taken a firm stand?

☐ Contacted your children's teacher if necessary?

SOLVING THE SEVEN MOST COMMON HOMEWORK PROBLEMS

Chapter 10

Solving the Seven Most Common Homework Problems

This chapter of *Homework Without Tears* pulls it all together to give you step-by-step solutions for the the seven most common homework problems. All of these solutions have been addressed in the previous chapters; they have been reorganized so that you can quickly pinpoint what needs to be done. Each problem is presented on an easy-to-follow worksheet. Page and chapter references are included for most of the steps so that you can easily review the information in greater detail if you so wish.

How to use this chapter:

Locate the problem you're having on the chart on page 94.

Turn to the page designated.

Read the description of the problem. Is this what's happening with your child? If the answer is "yes," read the step-by-step solutions listed on the worksheet. These are the steps you must follow to solve your child's particular problem with homework. Keep in mind that you will get the best results by using several (if not all) of the steps together.

The Seven Most Common Homework Problems

Problem #1   Child does not do his best work (i.e., the work is sloppy and full of mistakes). See page 95.

Problem #2   Child refuses to do homework assignments. See page 97.

Problem #3   Child fails to bring assignments home. See page 99.

Problem #4   Child takes all night to finish homework. See page 101.

Problem #5   Child will not do homework on his own. See page 103.

Problem #6   Child waits until the last minute to finish assignments. See page 105.

Problem #7   Child will not do homework if you're not home. See page 107.

PROBLEM # **1**

CHILD DOES NOT DO HIS BEST WORK

Unmotivated children do not put their best efforts into homework. They make only a minimum effort. They race through homework in order to move on to other, more enjoyable activities as quickly as possible. They are not concerned about doing a good job. Their work may be sloppy, badly prepared or full of mistakes.

Step-by-Step Solution

1

State clearly how you expect homework to be done.

Sit down with your child and tell him firmly and assertively, "I expect you to do each of your assignments to the best of your ability. Racing through your homework is not acceptable. Making so many mistakes is not acceptable. Sloppy, careless work is not acceptable."

2

Institute Mandatory Homework Time.

Take away your child's incentive to race through his homework. Require that he spend one-half hour to two hours each day (depending on his age) on academic activities. (See pages 27 - 28.)

3

Provide praise and positive support for your child each time he makes an effort to do his homework responsibly.

Make sure your child hears you say, "Great job getting all your homework done," "I like the way you've been getting right down to business when Daily Homework Time begins," etc. Find something to praise every day. (See Chapter 5.)

4

Provide additional incentives when appropriate.

You can often motivate children who resist homework with a backup reward system. Each time your child does his homework to the best of his ability (you establish the specific guidelines), let him earn a reward, or earn a point toward a prize. Use this system for at least a month to condition your child to a more positive attitude toward homework. (See Chapter 6.)

5

If all else fails, contact the teacher.

If the first four steps fail to motivate your child to approach his homework responsibly, contact the teacher. Get the teacher's input about the child's performance in school. Work together to come up with a plan to improve his motivation. (See Chapter 9.)

Keep this in mind :

You cannot allow your children to remain indifferent about their homework. If they develop such an unmotivated approach to learning, they are likely to have problems handling the "real world" as well.

CHILD REFUSES TO DO HOMEWORK ASSIGNMENTS

PROBLEM #2

Some children just don't do their homework. They battle with you about it every night. They may openly refuse to do it. They may lie to you about having done it. They may lie to the teacher about why they haven't done it.

Step-by-Step Solution

1

State clearly that you expect homework to be completed.

Sit down with your child and state clearly and assertively that you expect homework to be completed. Tell him, "We expect you to get all your homework done every night. Under no circumstances will we tolerate irresponsible behavior about homework."

2

Back up your words with action.

With most homework problems, you would want to motivate your child only through positive support. But when a child is engaged in a power struggle with you and openly refuses to do what you want, you must assert your authority if any impact is to be made. Tell your child:

"You have a choice. You can do your homework during Daily Homework Time or you can choose not to have privileges. If you choose not to do your homework, then from the beginning of Daily Homework Time until you have finished your homework you will lose these privileges: You will not leave this house. You will not watch TV. You will not listen to music. You will not be allowed to use the telephone, either to make or to receive calls. You will sit here until your homework is done. The choice is yours."

Follow through on your demands. It may take your child several days of sitting idly in his study area before he realizes you mean business. Be prepared for him to test your resolve through crying, becoming angry, or acting indifferent. (See Chapter 8.)

3

Contact the teacher. If appropriate, request that he or she provide additional discipline at school.

With a very difficult child, it may prove useful to involve the teacher in solving the homework problem. Ask him if he could follow up at school if your child does not finish the work at home. Your child will quickly learn the school is backing up your efforts. (See Chapter 9.)

4

Provide praise and positive support for your child when he does his homework.

Praise your child each time he does his homework. "I really like the way you've been getting your homework done. That's what I expect from you." (See Chapter 5)

5

Provide additional incentives when appropriate.

Once your child has started doing his homework on a regular basis, it may be useful to offer additional motivators to keep him on course. Offer small rewards and special privileges as incentives for continuing to do his homework responsibly. You may wish to use games and other structured activities as a framework for presenting these incentives.
(See Chapter 6.)

Keep this in mind:

Your children must learn that homework is not a battleground. There can be no power struggle over homework; it simply must be done. Your children must learn that conflict on this issue will not be tolerated.

PROBLEM #

CHILD FAILS TO BRING ASSIGNMENTS HOME

Some children frequently fail to bring home assigned homework. They may "forget" their homework. They may remember the assignment but "forget" their textbook in their locker. They may say they got the work done in study hall or at lunch period when in fact they have completed only part of it. In class the next day, the teacher hears a different set of excuses.

Step-by-Step Solution

1

State clearly that you expect all homework assignments to be brought home.

Sit down with your child and tell him clearly and assertively that you will not tolerate his forgetting to bring home his assignments. Tell him, "We expect you to get all assigned homework done every night. We expect you to bring home all your assigned work and all the books you need to complete your assignments. If you finish your homework during free time at school, we expect you to bring it home so that we can see it."

2

Work with the teacher to make sure you know what has been assigned.

It is a good idea to contact your child's teacher about his homework assignments. Insist that the child keep a homework log, and ask his teachers to support you in this effort by signing it every day.
(See Chapter 9.)

3

Institute Mandatory Homework Time.

Take away your child's incentive to "forget" his homework. He will not be as likely to leave it at school if he knows he is going to have to spend time on academic work whether he brings his work home or not .
(See pages 27 - 28.)

4

Provide praise and positive support when your child brings home all his homework.

Make sure your child knows that you appreciate his behavior every time he brings home all his homework. Praise his good efforts : "It's great to see you remembering to bring home all your homework. I knew you could do it!"

5

Provide additional incentives when appropriate.

If your child remains unmotivated about bringing his homework home, offer him small rewards or special privileges. For example, every evening that he brings all his work home, let him earn a point toward a prize. (See Chapter 6.)

6

If all else fails, work with the teacher to provide more severe consequences for inappropriate behavior.

If the first five steps fail to motivate your child to bring home all his homework, contact his teacher. Discuss with the teacher the possibility of his imposing additional consequences if the child continues to forget his homework. He may agree to take away the privilege of recess or of play at lunch hour, or to require him to complete the previous day's homework after school. Such support by the teacher lets your child know that home and school are working together to ensure that he behaves responsibly. (See Chapter 9.)

Keep this in mind:

Children must learn to bring home and complete all homework assignments. Accept no excuses.

CHILD TAKES ALL NIGHT TO FINISH HOMEWORK

PROBLEM # **4**

Some children take the entire evening to do their homework. They stop and start, and are easily distracted. They demand your assistance throughout the evening. As a result, you spend the entire evening battling with your children and feeling tense.

Step-by-Step Solution

1

State clearly that you expect all homework to be done during Daily Homework Time.

Sit down with your child and state clearly and assertively that you will not tolerate his taking all evening to do his homework: "We expect you to get all your homework done during Daily Homework Time. Your taking all evening to do it must stop at once." (See Chapter 3.)

2

Make sure that homework is being done in a proper study area.

Many children who take too much time to do their homework do so because they are working in a distracting environment. Make sure that during Daily Homework Time your child has no access to TV, stereo, or other distractions, and that he is not disturbed by brothers and sisters. You may wish to consider changing the location of his study area if such distractions are present. (See Chapter 2.)

3

Make yourself available for help only during Daily Homework Time.

To stop the continual interruptions and pleas for your help, let your child know that you will help him only during Daily Homework Time. The minute that the agreed-upon time period is over, your assistance will no longer be available, no matter how much difficulty he is having. Your child must learn that there are limits to your availability for help.

4
Provide praise and positive support when children do their homework on time.

Let your child feel your approval each time he finishes his homework during Daily Homework Time. Tell him promptly, "Great job! I'm really pleased to see that you got your homework done on time. I'm so proud of you!" (See Chapter 5.)

5
Provide additional incentives when appropriate.

Some children require additional incentives to help them develop the habit of getting their homework done without procrastinating. A good incentive for solving this particular problem is the "Beat the Clock" game. (See page 56.)

6
Back up your words with action.

If the first five steps do not succeed in getting your child to finish his homework during Daily Homework Time, you must take a stand. Tell your child: "You have a choice. You can do your homework during Daily Homework Time or you can choose not to have privileges. If you choose not to do your homework, then from the beginning of Daily Homework Time until you have finished your homework you will lose these privileges: You will not leave this house. You will not watch TV. You will not listen to music. You will not be allowed to use the telephone, either to make or to receive calls. You will sit there until your homework is done. The choice is yours." (See Chapter 8.)

Keep this in mind:

Your children must learn to do their homework responsibly. They must learn that there are limits to the help they can expect from you. They must learn to do their homework efficiently, productively, and on time.

PROBLEM # **5**

CHILD WILL NOT DO HOMEWORK ON HIS OWN

Some children will not do their homework on their own, even when they have the capability of doing so. Some children insist that you sit with them all night; others continually beg you for assistance.

Step-by-Step Solution

1

State clearly that you expect your child to work on his own.

Sit down with your child and tell him firmly and assertively that he is required to do his homework on his own: "We expect you to do your homework without our help. We are not responsible for doing your worksheets or writing your reports. We will not sit with you or do your homework for you. We will not be available to answer your questions every five minutes."

2

Help your child only after he has genuinely tried to solve the problem on his own.

Do not accede to your child's pleas for help until he has at least twice attempted to solve the problem or answer the question himself. Of course, there will be some times when something is legitimately too hard for him to understand. But be sure that you don't step in until he has made a genuine effort to do the work himself. (See Chapter 4.)

3

When a child does need help, use the process of encouragement to build his confidence.

When you do help your child, break an assignment down into small components that you know he can handle successfully. Work with him in a manner that will help him recognize his ability to do the work. Be sure to encourage him whenever he takes even the smallest step toward independence. (See pages 38 - 39.)

4

Provide praise and positive support whenever your child works on his own.

Monitor your child as he does his homework. When you see him working on his own, go to him promptly and let him know you like what he's doing: "I'm really proud of the way you're doing all this work on your own. I knew you could do it!" Be consistent with your praise.

5

Provide additional incentives when appropriate.

Some children need additional incentives to keep them working on their own. A good incentive for solving this particular problem is the "Trade Off!" game. (See page 58.)

6

Back up your words with action

If the first five steps do not succeed in getting your child to do his work on his own, it's time to get tough. Make sure your child knows that you will not help and that he will have to sit at his work space until his homework is done — even if it means he will remain there all evening. Be prepared for your child to use anger, tears, or indifference to try to manipulate you into backing down. Let him know beyond a doubt that such tactics will not work. He will still have to do his homework on his own, and you will follow through with the consequences until he learns to do so. (See Chapter 8.)

Keep this in mind:

Children must learn to do their homework on their own. Relying on you for help will only lead them to greater dependence. They must develop the confidence to tackle any homework assignment on their own.

PROBLEM # **6**

CHILD WAITS UNTIL THE LAST MINUTE TO FINISH ASSIGNMENTS

Some children put off starting long-range projects until just before they are due. Then they go into a frenzy, demanding your immediate help with their term paper or book report. Such behavior often puts stress on the entire family.

Step-by-Step Solution

1

State clearly that you expect long-range projects to be planned and completed responsibly.

Sit down with your child and tell him firmly and assertively that you will not tolerate his putting off long-range projects until just before they are due: "We expect you to plan your book reports (term papers, etc.) responsibly. This waiting until the last minute must stop."

2

Use the Long-Range Planner.

Read pages 122 - 123 of Chapter 11. Each time your child is given a long-range assignment, help him use the Long-Range Planner to plan his work. Insist that he tell you about each such assignment on the day it is given. Sit down with him and decide together when each step of the project is to be completed.

3

Monitor your child to make sure each step of the project is completed on time.

Check each day to make sure that progress is being made and that each step is being completed according to plan.

4

Provide praise and positive support for your child as each step is completed.

Each time your child completes a step of a long-range project, let him feel your approval: "I think it's wonderful that you picked out the book for your book report so quickly!" "I really like how you finished reading the book before the date you scheduled! Keep up the good work!"

5

Provide additional motivators when appropriate.

Some children may need additional incentives to motivate them to complete a long-range project on time. You may wish to institute a system that allows your child to earn a point toward a reward or privilege each time he completes a step of the project according to his schedule.

6

Back up your words with action.

If the first five steps fail to motivate your child to do long-range projects responsibly, it's time to impose restrictions. If the child fails to read a book selected for a book report by the agreed-upon date, take away a privilege (e.g., playing outside, watching TV) until he has read the book. Unless you set limits, he's not going to know that you mean business. (See Chapter 8.)

Keep this in mind:

Children must learn to budget the time allocated to them for long-range projects. It's a skill that they must develop if they are going to be capable of taking on larger and more complex tasks as they grow up.

PROBLEM # **7**

CHILD WILL NOT DO HOMEWORK IF YOU'RE NOT HOME

Some children will not do their homework unless a parent is there to watch over them. This can be a significant problem, especially in single-parent homes or in families where both parents work.

Step-by-Step Solution

1

State clearly that you expect homework to be done whether you're home or not.

Sit down with your child and let him know that you will not tolerate irresponsible behavior: "We expect you to get your homework done every night whether or not we are at home."

2

Make sure that the person responsible for child care knows about Daily Homework Time

It may be that your child is being cared for by a sitter or a relative, looked in on by a neighbor, or otherwise supervised by an adult in your absence. Make sure that this person knows where your child is expected to do homework (in his study area), when he is to do his homework (during Daily Homework Time — which should be posted), and how he is to do it (on his own). The involvement of the care-giver will depend upon the age of your child. It is a good idea to sit down together with your child and the person responsible for your child to communicate your expectation that homework will be done just as though you were home.

3

Monitor your children when you're not home to make sure homework is done.

Regardless of who is providing child care, it's a good idea for you to monitor your child to make sure he's doing his homework responsibly. Telephone at the beginning of Daily Homework Time to make sure he has begun his work. Call back, if possible, at the end of Daily Homework Time to make sure he has finished. Have him leave his homework out for you to check when you return home. You may phase out this monitoring when your child demonstrates that he's doing his work.

4

Provide praise and positive support.

Praise your child whenever he does his homework in your absence. When you call at the start of Daily Homework Time and find that he has started on time, tell him: "I really like the way you got started so promptly, even without my being there." When you get home and find that his work has been completed, let him know that you are pleased: "Great! You're doing such a good job on your homework when I'm not here. Keep up the good work!"

5

Use additional incentives when appropriate.

You may have to give your child additional incentives to get him to do his homework when you're not home. (One idea is to give him a Homework Contract (page 146) under which he earns a point toward a reward each time he does his homework in your absence.) Special incentives may be necessary at first to get your child into the habit of doing homework without your supervision.

6

Back up your words with action.

If the first five steps do not work, it's time to get tough. Tell your child that he is required to sit at his study area until his homework is finished, whether you are home or not. Tell your child: "You have a choice. You can do your homework during Daily Homework Time or you can choose not to have privileges. If you choose not to do your homework, then from the beginning of Daily Homework Time until you have finished your homework you will lose these privileges: You will not leave this house. You will not watch TV. You will not listen to music. You will not be allowed to use the telephone, either to make or to receive calls. You will sit there until your homework is finished. The choice is yours."

Don't back down! You may need to phone in frequently to monitor your child or to insist that the person providing child care enforces the rules.

If there is no one providing child care, you may have to impose backup disciplinary consequences as soon as you get home. Turn off the TV, get your child off the phone, and make sure that he gets back to work. You may have to have him complete or make up his homework over the weekend if there is no other time for him to do it. If all his weekend activities are suspended until his homework is completed, he will be more likely to be responsible next time.

Keep this in mind:

Regardless of whether or not you're home, children must learn that they are responsible for finishing their homework. They must learn that irresponsibility about homework is unacceptable.

Be sure to refer to The Seven Most Common Homework Problems anytime your children have difficulty getting homework assignments finished appropriately. By quickly identifying a specific problem — and taking the prescribed steps to solve it — you will get your children back on track and help ensure that homework problems will be resolved and not escalate into further difficulties.

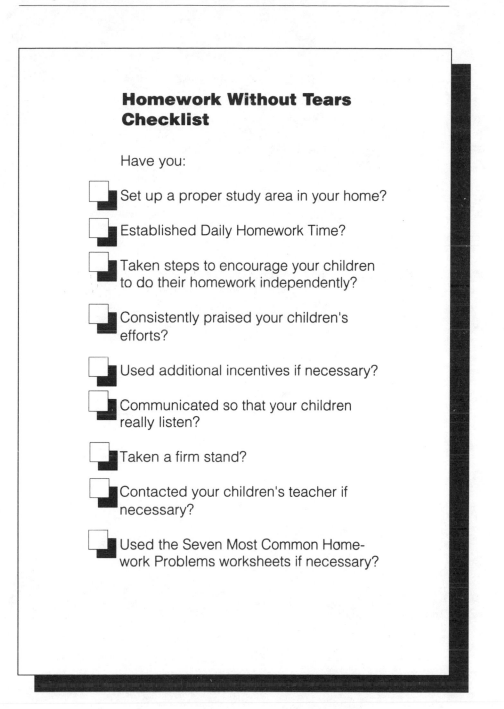

Homework Without Tears Checklist

Have you:

☐ Set up a proper study area in your home?

☐ Established Daily Homework Time?

☐ Taken steps to encourage your children to do their homework independently?

☐ Consistently praised your children's efforts?

☐ Used additional incentives if necessary?

☐ Communicated so that your children really listen?

☐ Taken a firm stand?

☐ Contacted your children's teacher if necessary?

☐ Used the Seven Most Common Homework Problems worksheets if necessary?

HOW TO HELP YOUR CHILDREN STUDY SUCCESSFULLY

Chapter 11

How to Help Your Children Study Successfully

Throughout *Homework Without Tears* you've learned that getting homework done responsibly takes more than just wishing it to happen. Your children need a proper study area, a designated homework time, consistent encouragement and motivation and, above all, a commitment on your part that homework is a priority in your home.

There's something else you can do to help your children work to their full capacity. You can encourage them to develop study skills.

As we mentioned in Chapter 1, study skills are techniques that enable students to learn more effectively. Knowing *how* to study is an essential component of successful learning. Students who know how to study manage their time to the best advantage. They get maximum return on their study investment. But good study habits don't just come naturally. They must be taught. Your children will be introduced to study skills in school. You can reinforce what they learn by encouraging your children to make full use of these skills. In this chapter, *Homework Without Tears* provides a set of study skills that will help your children do their homework—and assignments in class—more effectively.

Study Skills

TIPS FOR READING

Children who have strong reading skills are well prepared for success in all subject areas. As a parent, there are many things you can do to help your children acquire these skills. You're not expected to teach them to read, but you can provide an environment in which reading is a valued—and shared—activity.

Keep in mind that one of the most important things you can do to encourage your children to read is to be a reader yourself. When children grow up seeing their parents enjoying reading, they will naturally develop some curiosity about it. Reading materials, then, should be as much a part of your home as the TV set or the stereo.

The following list of suggestions is designed to enhance the "reading environment" of your home.

Read to your children.

One of the best things you can do to encourage your children to read is to read to them. Start when they're very young and continue as long as they want to listen.

Listen to your children read aloud.

Children love to read to their parents. It builds their sense of pride and increases reading skills. (Reading out loud gives children the opportunity to pay particular attention to punctuation and inflection.) Be careful not to be critical when your children read. Remember, you want this to be a pleasurable activity.

Make regular visits to the library with your children.

Get acquainted with the children's section of your library. Many wonderful books are available for all levels of young readers. The librarian can help you and your children pick out ones that are appropriate. In addition, libraries often sponsor children's reading clubs and story hours. Take advantage of these programs.

Help your children get a library card of their own.

"Ownership" of a library card helps develop a sense of responsibility and pride in children. Emphasize that, with their signature, your children are promising to abide by the rules of the library and to take care of the books they borrow.

Help your children build up a library of their own.

Few things are quite as satisfying for children as having their own collection of treasured books. (Very often these books will be kept a lifetime, continuing to give pleasure to newer generations.)   Books don't have to be expensive. Here are some sources:

- School book fairs
- Library sales (of discarded books)
- Garage sales
- Book clubs

Give your children a gift subscription to a magazine.

There are many excellent magazines written expecially for children. (Check out the selection in the children's section of your library.) Many of these magazines cater to specific interests, so you should be able to find something that will particularly interest your children: crafts, computers, games, literature, history, fashion, etc.

Encourage children to write stories of their own.

Many children who enjoy reading (or listening to stories) also like to write — and illustrate — stories of their own. If your children are young, have them dictate their stories to you. You can write your child's story down, one or two printed sentences to a page, staple them together, and give the story back to her to illustrate. The finished product is sure to become a favorite "read-along" story. Encourage older children to write by having supplies available (pens, pencils, lined and plain paper, marking pens) and, most importantly, by reading and appreciating the results.

Turn off the TV and read—together.

Some families find that a "reading hour" can be a welcome and peaceful addition to the end of a busy day. The value you place on reading is reinforced by the fact that you are reading along with your children. In addition, it's a good time for children to share their thoughts about the books they are currently reading.

POWER READING

Strong reading comprehension skills are the basis for success in all subject areas.   You can help your children develop these skills with Power Reading.   Power Reading is a technique that will help your children become better readers by increasing both reading comprehension and listening comprehension skills. A Power Reading session takes only about fifteen minutes.

Here's how to do it:

1. Read to your child.

Read aloud to your child for five minutes. (Be sure that the book from which you are reading is at your child's reading level.) Pronounce words carefully and clearly, and make appropriate pauses for periods and commas.

2. Listen to your child read.

Have your child continue reading the same book aloud (He should begin at the point where you stopped reading.) Remind your child to take it slowly and read so that what he is saying makes sense. (That's why your oral reading is so important—it's setting an example for your child.) Caution: Do not stop and correct your child while he is reading. If he stumbles on a word, make a note of it and go back later.

3. Ask questions about the material that was read.

Check how well your child was listening and reading by asking general questions about the material *you* read aloud and the material *he* read aloud. Talk about his responses; share ideas.

Hold a Power Reading session with your child as often as possible. It's an excellent way to improve reading skills *and* an excellent way to demonstrate the importance you place on reading. Many families have found Power Reading to be an entertaining way to read together on a regular basis. Start a book that's of particular interest to your child and continue using this same book for Power Reading sessions until it is completed. Your child will be even more motivated to join you in Power Reading when he's eager to "find out what happens next."

TIPS FOR PREPARING FOR SPELLING TESTS

Most children have weekly spelling tests throughout elementary school. The spelling assignments are usually given on Monday, but all too often children don't begin studying until the night before the test. Here are some easy techniques to help your children successfully study throughout the week for spelling tests .

Monday

Make spelling flashcards. Have your child write each of her spelling words on a 3" x 5" index card.

Tuesday

Sit down with your child and practice the spelling words.
Follow this sequence with each flashcard:

1. Have your child carefully look at the word.
2. Have your child say the word.
3. Have your child use the word in a sentence.
4. Have your child spell the word out loud while looking at the flashcard.

Wednesday

Follow this sequence with each flashcard:

1. Have your child look at the word.
2. Have your child say the word.
3. After your child has said the word, ask her to turn the flashcard face down and spell the word aloud.
4. After spelling the word aloud, ask your child to turn over the flashcard and check for spelling accuracy.
5. Place the flashcards of any misspelled words in a separate pile.

Have your child write each misspelled word several times on a separate sheet of paper.

Thursday

Give your child a practice test. Follow these guidelines:

1. Give your child a sheet of lined paper.
2. Dictate each spelling word to your child. Allow her time to write the word.
3. When you have completed the practice test, have your child use her flashcards to correct her work.
4. Place the flashcards of any misspelled words in a separate pile. Have your child write each of these words several times on a separate sheet of paper.

Here's a great idea: If your child has a tape recorder, have her dictate her spelling words aloud. Then she can play back the tape and take the spelling test—all on her own.

Note: Don't throw away the spelling flashcards! Have your children keep each week's spelling flashcards in a "Spelling Words" box. Keep them available to study for spelling review tests.

HOW TO HELP WITH LONG-RANGE PLANNING

In addition to regularly assigned daily homework, children receive long-range assignments such as book reports, term papers, and studying for tests. These long-range assignments are often overwhelming because children do not know how to structure their time in order to get the work done. Most children leave the bulk of the work to do at the last minute.

A Long-Range Planner can teach your children how to successfully complete longer projects. By using the Long-Range Planner, your children will learn how to break down an overwhelming project into small, easily completed tasks. They will learn how to distribute the assignment over the period of time given for the project, and how to complete it on time. Make copies of the Long-Range Planner on page 149 of the Appendix. Keep these copies handy for use whenever your children bring home long-range projects.

Note: Your child's teacher may assign due dates for various steps of a long-range project. You can incorporate these dates into the Long-Range Planner included in this book, or utilize whatever form the teacher may send home. In any case, the goal is the same—to help your child complete long-range projects on time.

Using the Long-Range Planner

When your child brings home a long-range project, sit down and help him determine the steps he'll have to follow to complete the project. Once you and your child have broken down the assignment into more easily managed steps, work together to establish the time period in which each of the steps will be completed. Write down the steps and the dates of completion on the Long-Range Planner. (The example on the next page shows a completed Long-Range Planner for a term report.) If each time goal is met, there will be no last-minute panic before the report is due.

Sometimes it is useful to break down each step into even smaller parts. For example, if a book to be read for a book report is 200 pages long, and the child has allowed himself 17 days in which to read it, help him plan to read a minimum of 12 pages each day.

Note: Your involvement in helping your children organize long-range projects will depend upon their age and the degree to which they have successfully worked independently. As your children become familiar with the Long-Range Planner, encourage them to plan the steps of their projects by themselves.

LONG-RANGE PLANNER

NAME _____ DATE Jan. 28

ASSIGNMENT _Term Report_ DUE DATE March 6

STEP 1	Pick out topic of the report.	Date to be completed Feb. 2
STEP 2	Do fact-finding research.	Date to be completed Feb. 11
STEP 3	Decide what questions I want to answer in the report.	Date to be completed Feb. 15
STEP 4	Take notes about the topic.	Date to be completed Feb. 22
STEP 5	Write the rough draft.	Date to be completed Feb. 29
STEP 6	Write the final draft.	Date to be completed March 6
STEP 7		Date to be completed
STEP 8		Date to be completed

HOW TO HELP YOUR CHILD WITH WRITTEN REPORTS

By the time they reach fourth grade, most children are assigned written reports on a regular basis. These reports are often difficult for children to handle in an organized manner. Here are some tips that will help you encourage your children in doing their best work.

TIP #1: Use the Long-Range Planner.

As stated in the previous section, planning is a critical part of getting a written report done on time. If your child leaves a book report or term paper until the last minute, it is very unlikely that she will do her best work. She will be too rushed and hassled. Use of the Long - Range Planner will ensure that the project will be thought out and pursued in an organized manner.

TIP #2: Use the Written Report Checklist.

Before your child writes a report, make sure she completes the Written Report Checklist. (Make copies of the Checklist on page 150 of the Appendix.)   By answering these questions before she starts to write, your child will prevent many unnecessary errors and rewrites.

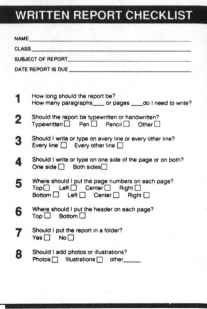

TIP #3:   Use Proofreading Checklists.

Proofreading is a critical step in completing any written assignment. You can help your child develop important proofreading skills by providing a Proofreading Checklist (see pages 151 - 153 of the Appendix). Make enough copies of the Checklist so that there will always be plenty availlable in your child's Homework Survival Kit. Be sure to use the Proofreading Checklist appropriate for your child's grade.

Follow these guidelines for using the Proofreading Checklists:

Grades 1-3

Your child will need your assistance in using the Checklist.

Sit down together with both her written assignment and the Checklist. Read each item on the Checklist aloud. Ask your child to answer "yes" or "no" to each statement.

Go slowly. Allow your child enough time for careful checking.

If your child answers "no" to any statements, have her correct the work, then check it again.

Grades 4-6

When using it for the first time, go over the Proofreading Checklist with your child, making sure that she understands each of the statements listed.

Encourage your child to then use the Checklist on her own and make all necessary corrections to her written assignment.

Tell your child that she should use the Proofreading Checklist after each draft of a written assignment.

Until your child is comfortable with this proofreading process, look over the completed Checklist and subsequent corrections your child has made.

Make sure your child has a supply of Proofreading Checklists available in her Homework Survival Kit.

Grades 7-12

Give your child a supply of Proofreading Checklists to keep in her Homework Survival Kit. Your child should be able to use the Checklist on her own. Give assistance if needed. Make sure that she understands that each draft of a written assignment should be proofread.

STEPS FOR WRITING A TERM REPORT

Term reports really test a child's organizational and time-management skills. *Homework Without Tears'* Steps for Writing a Term Report will help your child tackle the job in an orderly and comprehensive manner.

Step 1   Pick an appropriate topic.

Step 2   Do fact-finding research.

Step 3   Determine questions you want to answer about the topic.

Step 4   Take notes about the topic.

Step 5   Write an outline of the report.

Step 6   Write a rough draft of the report. Check for accuracy and make corrections as needed.

Step 7   Write the final draft of the report.

Before you begin:

Give your child a copy of the Long-Range Planner (page 149 of the Appendix). Make sure he fills in each of the steps listed for writing a term report, plus projected completion dates. Using the Long-Range Planner will ensure that the term report is finished on time and in an organized manner.

Give your child a copy of the Written Report Checklist (page 150 of the Appendix). By completing this Checklist your child will make certain that the report is organized as instructed.

Step 1 Pick an appropriate topic.

Encourage your child to pick a topic in which he is really interested. The more intriguing he finds the topic, the more motivated he will be to do the report. Be sure the topic is of a managable size. For example, "weather" is too broad a topic. Instead, a report could be narrowed down to "major storms," or, more specifically, "hurricanes."

Step 2 Do fact-finding research.

After your child has chosen a topic, he needs to begin researching it.

He should start with general information reference books to get a broad idea of the information on the topic. Such books include encyclopedias, atlases, and almanacs.

After gathering general information on the topic, your child needs to compile more specific facts. Now he must find books written specifically on the topic, for example, books on hurricanes. Research may also include newspaper and magazine articles on the topic.

**Step 3   Determine questions you want to answer
about the topic.**

As your child begins researching the facts for a report, he needs to determine the questions he wants answered. What does he want to learn about the topic? For example, here are some questions a child might want answered about hurricanes:

> What is a hurricane?
> What causes hurricanes?
> Where do hurricanes occur?
> Can hurricanes be predicted?
> How destructive are hurricanes?

Step 4 Take notes about the topic.

Doing research means finding facts. And finding facts means your child must take notes so that he can retain those facts and use them later. The best way to take notes is to use 3" x 5" index cards.

Tell your child that whenever he finds information he needs, he should write it down on an index card. In addition, he should write down the source (for example, book title and page number) so he can go back for further reference when necessary.

In addition to filling out the index cards, your child may want to complete a chart listing the information he has researched related to his questions. (See page 154 of the Appendix for Written Report Information Chart.) On the top of the chart the child should list the questions he wants to answer. On the left hand column of the chart, have the child list the sources. Then have him fill in brief information on each source. At the bottom of the page, have him fill in conclusions that have been found related to the questions. Make copies of this chart and keep them handy for your child to use.

WRITTEN REPORT INFORMATION CHART

	QUESTION 1 What is a hurricane?	QUESTION 2	QUESTION 3
SOURCE Encyclopedia	A tropical cyclone with winds over 74 mph.		
SOURCE "Hurricanes" by J. Brady	A low pressure area accompanied by heavy rainfall.		
SOURCE "Tropical Storms" by G. Smith	Hurricanes usually cover an area of 200-400 miles in diameter.		
	CONCLUSION 1 A hurricane is a tropical cyclone of winds over 74 mph, accompanied by heavy rain and covering an area of 200-400 miles in diameter.	CONCLUSION 2	CONCLUSION 3

Step 5   Write an outline of the report.

An outline is a guide used to write a report. The outline should be written so that the topic covered is clear to anyone who reads it.

Step 6   Write a rough draft of the report.

Have your child use a Proofreading Checklist to make certain he's done his best work. (See pages 151 - 153 of the Appendix for Proof-reading Checklists.) Make corrections as needed.

Step 7   Write a final draft of the report.

Have your child use the Written Report Checklist that he filled in before beginning the term report to make sure that his report is organized as instructed. He should then use the appropriate Proof-reading Checklist (pages 151 - 153 of the Appendix) to give the re-port a final inspection.

HOW TO HELP YOUR CHILD STUDY FOR TESTS

PART ONE: WHAT TO DO BEFORE YOUR CHILD BEGINS STUDYING FOR A TEST

Step 1   Determine what the test will cover.

Your child needs to know exactly what material the test will cover: chapters in the textbook, class notes, homework assignments, etc. Make copies of the Test Study Sheet on page 155 of the Appendix. Keep these copies handy for use whenever your child knows a test is coming up. Tell your child to fill in the sheet completely as soon as a test is scheduled.

Step 2   Organize all study material.

Your child will study more effectively if she has organized all the material that will be covered in the test.   Make sure she has completed any missed assignments and received any information covered on days she was absent.

Your child should use the Test Study Sheet to help organize all necessary materials.

TEST STUDY SHEET

NAME_____

TOPIC OF TEST_____

DATE OF TEST_____

1. In the spaces below, list all the material you need to study for the test.
2. Check off each box in the Study Complete column when you know the material.

MATERIAL TO STUDY

	STUDY COMPLETED
CHAPTERS IN TEXTBOOK	☐
CLASS NOTES, From (date)	☐
HOMEWORK ASSIGNMENTS	☐
PAST QUIZZES or TESTS	☐
OTHER	☐

Step 3 Schedule time for studying.

Your child needs to plan her study time carefully to make sure she allows enough time to prepare for the test. Make copies of the Test Study Planner on page 156 of the Appendix. The Study Planner will enable your child to block out needed study time and keep track of the progress she's making as she approaches the test date.

Step 4 Use effective study techniques.

The following study techniques can help your child study more effectively:

TEST STUDY PLANNER

NAME _____
TOPIC OF TEST _____ DATE OF TEST _____
MATERIAL TO STUDY
TEXTBOOK, Chapters _____
CLASS NOTES, From (date): _____
HOMEWORK, From (date): _____
PAST QUIZZES or TESTS _____
OTHER _____
_____

DAYS UNTIL TEST **MATERIAL TO STUDY**
10 _____
9 _____
8 _____
7 _____
6 _____
5 _____
4 _____
3 _____
2 _____
1 _____

Write important information on index cards.

Keep 3"x 5" index cards available at home. (They should always be kept in your child's Homework Survival Kit.) As your child studies, she should summarize important information in her own words and write it on index cards. Later, these index cards can be used to review for the test.

Review homework and class notes.

Your child should review all homework and class notes before a test. It is helpful to underline or highlight important points. Some children use different colored highlighters to organize or prioritize material from their notes and homework.

Review study questions, past quizzes and tests.

Encourage your child to look over past tests and quizzes. They might give clues about what he can expect on future tests. Did the teacher ask multiple choice questions? True/False questions? Essay questions? Was he or she interested in names and dates, or general trends? Make sure your child also spends time reviewing the study questions in the textbook. These questions generally provide an excellent review of the material covered.

Make a list of sample test questions.

Have your child make up a list of test questions that she thinks might show up on the test. Then have her prepare answers for these questions. Chances are, a lot of the questions *will* be given on the test.

PART TWO: HOW TO STUDY INFORMATION IN A TEXTBOOK

Often most of the material covered on a test will be from assigned reading in the class textbook. Many children, however, have never been taught how to study a chapter in a textbook for a test. In this section we will present ideas that will enable your children to master the material in any textbook.

Before you begin: Make copies of the How to Study Information in a Textbook Checklist on page 157 of the Appendix. Give this checklist to your child to help him keep track of the steps he should take in studying his textbook for a test.

Step 1   Survey the chapter.

The first step in studying a textbook is to survey the chapter. Have your child follow these steps:

1. Make note of the headings of each main section.
2. Look over all pictures, maps, charts, tables, and graphs.
3. Read the summary at the end of the chapter.
4. Read through the study questions listed at the end of the chapter.
5. Finally, go back and formulate a question from each main heading. For example, if the heading is "The Declaration of In-dependence," you should ask, "What is the Declaration of In-dependence?" As you read the chapter (see Step 2) you will attempt to answer these questions.

Step 2   Read the chapter and take notes.

After your child has surveyed the chapter, he should go back and read it all the way through. As your child reads, he should make notes on a separate sheet of paper. These notes should include:

> Answers to the questions he formulated from the chapter headings. A chronological listing of events that occur in the chapter. (This is especially important in social studies and history.)

In addition, your child should take notes on index cards. On the front of the cards he should list important facts: names of persons, terms to know, or significant concepts. On the back of the cards he should list important points that may be asked on the test.

Step 3   Review the chapter.

After your child finishes reading the chapter, he should look over his notes and make sure he understands all the main points and how they interrelate. Then he should answer the study questions given at the end of the chapter, as well as the questions he formulated from the main headings. He should review all his notes and all the key points of the chapter.

By using the How to Study Information in a Textbook Checklist, and by following these three steps, your child should be well prepared to answer test questions pertaining to textbook material.

It is important that you continue to reinforce your children's use of the study skills presented in this chapter. By making the study skills worksheets readily available—and by encouraging your children to use them—you are helping them manage their time effectively, organize their work, and approach school in a positive, more confident manner. And that's what success in school is all about!

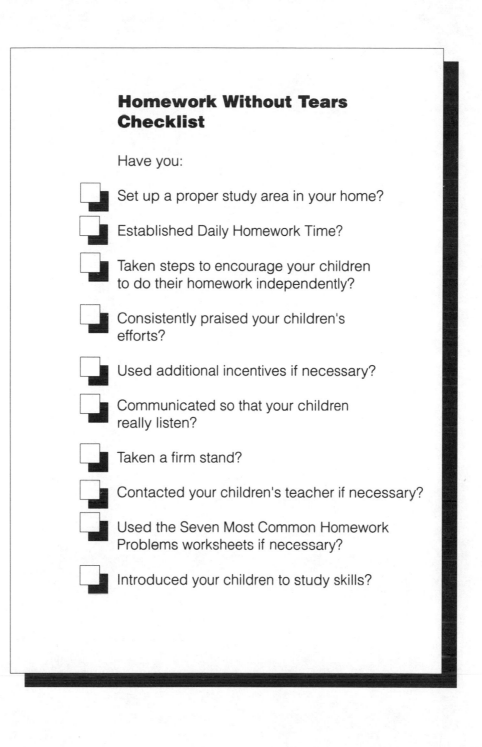

Homework Without Tears Checklist

Have you:

☐ Set up a proper study area in your home?

☐ Established Daily Homework Time?

☐ Taken steps to encourage your children to do their homework independently?

☐ Consistently praised your children's efforts?

☐ Used additional incentives if necessary?

☐ Communicated so that your children really listen?

☐ Taken a firm stand?

☐ Contacted your children's teacher if necessary?

☐ Used the Seven Most Common Homework Problems worksheets if necessary?

☐ Introduced your children to study skills?

CONCLUSION

Homework is all about your children learning to make choices: *when* to do homework, *how* to do homework, *where* to do homework, and even *if* they will do homework.

It is, therefore, in their best interest that they learn to make these choices intelligently. That's why laying a proper study foundation is so important. By teaching your children basic organizational skills and improving their study habits you are giving them the tools that will help them make good choices about schoolwork. They will understand that with a little planning they *can* deal successfully with homework, do better in school, and feel better about themselves.

Practical knowledge plus increased self-esteem.It's a winning combination that will help your children make choices that are good for them—both in school and later in life. It is our hope that *Homework Without Tears* has given you, and will continue to give you, the support you need to make homework success a reality in your home.

APPENDIX

The Appendix of *Homework Without Tears* contains all of the worksheets that have been demonstrated throughout this book. We know that you will find them useful as you implement the *Homework Without Tears* program in your own home. You may make as many copies of these worksheets as you wish as often as you need them.

DAILY SCHEDULE

MONDAY / HOMEWORK TIME:

3:00 PM	7:00 PM
4:00 PM	8:00 PM
5:00 PM	9:00 PM
6:00 PM	10:00 PM

TUESDAY / HOMEWORK TIME:

3:00 PM	7:00 PM
4:00 PM	8:00 PM
5:00 PM	9:00 PM
6:00 PM	10:00 PM

WEDNESDAY / HOMEWORK TIME:

3:00 PM	7:00 PM
4:00 PM	8:00 PM
5:00 PM	9:00 PM
6:00 PM	10:00 PM

THURSDAY / HOMEWORK TIME:

3:00 PM	7:00 PM
4:00 PM	8:00 PM
5:00 PM	9:00 PM
6:00 PM	10:00 PM

FRIDAY / HOMEWORK TIME:

3:00 PM	7:00 PM
4:00 PM	8:00 PM
5:00 PM	9:00 PM
6:00 PM	10:00 PM

WEEKLY PLANNER

NAME_____ DATE_____

SUBJECTS	MONDAY	TUESDAY	WEDNESDAY	THURSDAY	FRIDAY

is a

Homework Super Star

HOMEWORK CONTRACT

- Each day that you complete all your homework assignments, check off one square.

- When you have checked off _____ squares, you will earn a reward.

- Your reward will be _____

_____

_____   _____
PARENT'S SIGNATURE   STUDENT'S SIGNATURE

Expiration Date_____

ELEMENTARY HOMEWORK LOG

NAME _____

DATE _____

SUBJECT	HOMEWORK ASSIGNMENT	TEACHER'S SIGNATURE

148

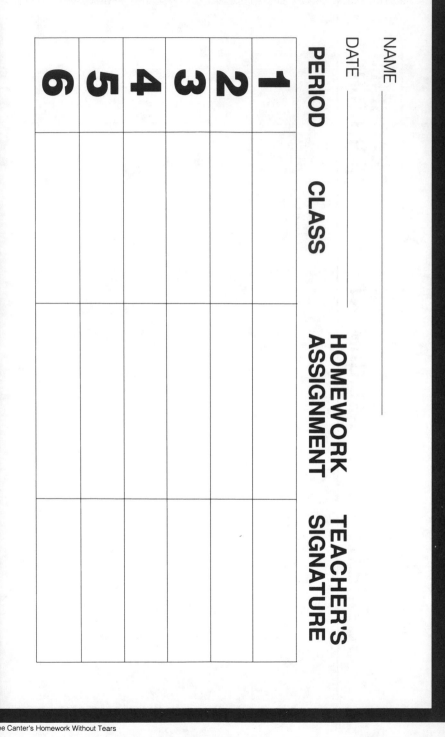

HOMEWORK ASSIGNMENT LOG

NAME _____

DATE _____

PERIOD	CLASS	HOMEWORK ASSIGNMENT	TEACHER'S SIGNATURE
1			
2			
3			
4			
5			
6			

LONG-RANGE PLANNER

NAME_____ DATE_____

ASSIGNMENT_____ DUE DATE_____

STEP 1
_____ Date to be completed _____
_____

STEP 2
_____ Date to be completed _____
_____

STEP 3
_____ Date to be completed _____
_____

STEP 4
_____ Date to be completed _____
_____

STEP 5
_____ Date to be completed _____
_____

STEP 6
_____ Date to be completed _____
_____

STEP 7
_____ Date to be completed _____
_____

STEP 8
_____ Date to be completed _____
_____

WRITTEN REPORT CHECKLIST

NAME _____

CLASS _____

SUBJECT OF REPORT _____

DATE REPORT IS DUE _____

1 How long should the report be?
How many paragraphs____ or pages ____do I need to write?

2 Should the report be typewritten or handwritten?
Typewritten ☐   Pen ☐   Pencil ☐   Other ☐

3 Should I write or type on every line or every other line?
Every line ☐   Every other line ☐

4 Should I write or type on one side of the page or on both?
One side ☐   Both sides ☐

5 Where should I put the page numbers on each page?
Top ☐   Left ☐   Center ☐   Right ☐
Bottom ☐   Left ☐   Center ☐   Right ☐

6 Where should I put the header on each page?
Top ☐   Bottom ☐

7 Should I put the report in a folder?
Yes ☐   No ☐

8 Should I add photos or illustrations?
Photos ☐   Illustrations ☐   other_____

PROOFREADING CHECKLIST

Grades 1 - 3

- [ ] My printing (or handwriting) is neat and readable.

- [ ] My paper has a title (if needed).

- [ ] I have said what I wanted to say.

- [ ] Each sentence begins with a capital letter.

- [ ] Each sentence ends with a period, a question mark, or an exclamation point.

- [ ] Every sentence is a complete sentence.

- [ ] I have checked for spelling mistakes.

- [ ] This is my best work.

PROOFREADING CHECKLIST

Grades 4 - 6

- [ ] My handwriting is neat and readable.

- [ ] The title of the paper is suited to the subject.

- [ ] I have put in all capital letters, commas, periods and apostrophes where needed.

- [ ] Every sentence is a complete sentence.

- [ ] Each paragraph has a topic sentence that tells what the paragraph will be about.

- [ ] I have used descriptive words to make my paper more interesting.

- [ ] I have read my paper out loud, and it says what I want it to say.

- [ ] The last sentence of the paper lets the reader know that the paper is finished.

- [ ] I have checked the paper for spelling errors.

- [ ] This is my best work.

PROOFREADING CHECKLIST

Grades 7 - 12

☐ The paper is well organized with a clear introduction.

☐ Each paragraph has a topic sentence. Every sentence within the paragraph is related to that topic sentence.

☐ The paper contains specific facts and information as needed.

☐ I have checked the paper for punctuation. Commas, periods, apostrophes, semicolons and quotation marks are all properly located and marked.

☐ I have capitalized words as needed.

☐ I have used descriptive words to make my paper more interesting and more accurate.

☐ I have checked for run-on sentences and incomplete sentences.

☐ I have checked for spelling errors.

☐ I have done at least one draft of the paper.

☐ I have chosen an appropriate title for the paper.

☐ This is my best work.

154

WRITTEN REPORT INFORMATION CHART

	QUESTION 1	QUESTION 2	QUESTION 3
SOURCE			
SOURCE			
SOURCE			
	CONCLUSION 1	CONCLUSION 2	CONCLUSION 3

TEST STUDY SHEET

NAME_____

TOPIC OF TEST_____

DATE OF TEST_____

1. In the spaces below, list all the material
   you need to study for the test.

2. Check off each box in the Study Completed
   column when you know the material.

MATERIAL TO STUDY

STUDY
COMPLETED

CHAPTERS IN TEXTBOOK _____ ☐

_____

CLASS NOTES, From (date) _____ ☐

_____

HOMEWORK ASSIGNMENTS _____ ☐

_____

_____

_____

PAST QUIZZES or TESTS _____ ☐

_____

_____

_____

OTHER _____ ☐

_____

_____

_____

_____

TEST STUDY PLANNER

NAME_____

TOPIC OF TEST_____ DATE OF TEST_____

MATERIAL TO STUDY

TEXTBOOK, Chapters_____

CLASS NOTES, From (date):_____

HOMEWORK, From (date):_____

PAST QUIZZES or TESTS_____

OTHER_____

_____

DAYS UNTIL TEST **MATERIAL TO STUDY**

10 _____

9 _____

8 _____

7 _____

6 _____

5 _____

4 _____

3 _____

2 _____

1 _____

HOW TO STUDY INFORMATION IN A TEXTBOOK *CHECKLIST*

NAME _____

TEXTBOOK _____

CHAPTER _____

1 Survey the chapter.

As I surveyed the chapter, I
- [ ] Noted all major headings.
- [ ] Noted all pictures, maps, charts, tables, graphs, etc.
- [ ] Read the summary at the end of the chapter.
- [ ] Read the study questions listed at the end of the chapter.

2 Make questions of major headings.

- [ ] I went through the chapter and reworded all main headings into study questions I will answer.

3 Read the chapter and take notes.

As I read the chapter, I
- [ ] Answered all the questions I made of the main headings.
- [ ] Took notes on a separate piece of paper.
- [ ] Listed important events, concepts, or facts in order.
- [ ] Made 3"x5" index cards of important terms, people and events.

4 Review the chapter.

As I reviewed the chapter, I
- [ ] Made sure I understood all the main points and how they relate to one another.
- [ ] Answered all the study questions at the end of the chapter.
- [ ] Reviewed notes to make sure I covered all key points.